*Where do I go for answers to my travel questions?*

*What's the best and easiest way to plan and book my trip?*

# frommers.travelocity.com

**Frommer's**, the travel guide leader, has teamed up with **Travelocity.com,** the leader in online travel, to bring you an in-depth, easy-to-use resource designed to help you plan and book your trip online.

At **frommers.travelocity.com**, you'll find free online updates about your destination from the experts at Frommer's plus the outstanding travel planning and purchasing features of Travelocity.com. Travelocity.com provides reservations capabilities for 95 percent of all airline seats sold, more than 47,000 hotels, and over 50 car rental companies. In addition, Travelocity.com offers more than 2,000 exciting vacation and cruise packages. Travelocity.com puts you in complete control of your travel planning with these and other great features:

> **Expert travel guidance from Frommer's** - over 150 writers reporting from around the world!

> **Best Fare Finder** - an interactive calendar tells you when to travel to get the best airfare

> **Fare Watcher** - we'll track airfare changes to your favorite destinations

> **Dream Maps** - a mapping feature that suggests travel opportunities based on your budget

> **Shop Safe Guarantee** - 24 hours a day / 7 days a week live customer service, and more!

Whether traveling on a tight budget, looking for a quick weekend getaway, or planning the trip of a lifetime, Frommer's guides and Travelocity.com will make your travel dreams a reality. You've bought the book, now book the trip!

## Here's what the critics say about Frommer's:

"Amazingly easy to use. Very portable, very complete."

—*Booklist*

♦

"The only mainstream guide to list specific prices. The Walter Cronkite of guidebooks—with all that implies."

—*Travel & Leisure*

♦

"Complete, concise, and filled with useful information."

—*New York Daily News*

♦

"Hotel information is close to encyclopedic."

—*Des Moines Sunday Register*

♦

"Detailed, accurate and easy-to-read information for all price ranges."

—*Glamour*

# Rocky Mountain National Park

## 2nd Edition

### by Don & Barbara Laine

HUNGRY MINDS, INC.
New York, NY • Cleveland, OH • Indianapolis, IN

## ABOUT THE AUTHORS

Residents of northern New Mexico for over 30 years, **Don and Barbara Laine** have traveled extensively throughout the Rocky Mountains and the Southwest, spending as much time as possible in the region's national parks and monuments. In addition to this book, they have authored or contributed to numerous travel guides, including *Frommer's Colorado, Frommer's Denver, Boulder & Colorado Springs, Frommer's Utah, Frommer's Texas, Frommer's Zion & Bryce Canyon National Parks,* and *Frommer's National Parks of the American West.*

Published by:

**HUNGRY MINDS, INC.**
909 Third Avenue
New York, NY 10022
**www.frommers.com**

ISBN 0-7645-6341-6
ISSN 1523-3901

Editor: Paul E. Kruger
Production Editor: Todd A. Siesky
Photo Editor: Richard Fox
Design by Michele Laseau
Staff Cartographer: Roberta Stockwell
Additional cartography: Barbara Laine
Production by Hungry Minds Indianapolis Production Services

## SPECIAL SALES

For general information on Hungry Minds' products and services please contact our Customer Care department; within the U.S. at 800-762-2974, outside the U.S. at 317-572-3993 or fax 317-572-4002. For sales inquiries and reseller information, including discounts, bulk sales, customized editions, and premium sales, please contact our Customer Care department at 800-434-3422.

Manufactured in the United States of America

5  4  3  2  1

# Contents

## 4    Hikes & Other Outdoor Pursuits in Rocky Mountain National Park    64

## 5    Camping in Rocky Mountain National Park    103

## 6    Gateway Towns & the National Forests    113

# List of Maps

## ACKNOWLEDGMENTS

The authors wish to thank for their help: Dick Putney at Rocky Mountain National Park and Suzy Blackhurst at Market Reach in Estes Park.

## AN INVITATION TO THE READER

In researching this book we discovered many wonderful places—hotels, restaurants, shops, and more. We're sure you'll find others. Please tell us about them, so we can share the information with your fellow travelers in upcoming editions. If you were disappointed with a recommendation, we'd love to know that, too. Please write to:

*Frommer's Rocky Mountain National Park,* 2nd Edition
Hungry Minds, Inc.
909 Third Avenue
New York, NY 10022

## AN ADDITIONAL NOTE

Please be advised that travel information is subject to change at any time—and this is especially true of prices. We therefore suggest that you write or call ahead for confirmation when making your travel plans. The authors, editors, and publisher cannot be held responsible for the experiences of readers while traveling. Your safety is important to us, however, so we encourage you to stay alert and be aware of your surroundings. Keep a close eye on cameras, purses, and wallets, all favorite targets of thieves and pickpockets.

## WHAT THE SYMBOLS MEAN

### ✪ Frommer's Favorites

Our favorite places and experiences—outstanding for quality, value, or both.
The following abbreviations are used for credit cards:

| | | | |
|---|---|---|---|
| AE | American Express | DISC | Discover |
| CB | Carte Blanche | MC | MasterCard |
| DC | Diners Club | V | Visa |

## FIND FROMMER'S ONLINE

**www.frommers.com** offers up-to-the-minute listings on almost 200 cities around the globe—including the latest bargains and candid, personal articles updated daily by Arthur Frommer himself. No other Web site offers such comprehensive and timely coverage of the world of travel.

## ILLUSTRATION CREDITS

Line drawings on pages 156 (Ponderosa pine, Quaking aspen), 157 (Alpine sunflower), 158 (Colorado columbine, Elephant heads), 160 (Sky pilot), 164 (American beaver, Least chipmunk), 168 (Mountain lion), 171 (Yellow-bellied marmot, Broad-tailed hummingbird), 173 (Steller's jay, Mallard, Mountain bluebird), and 175 (Violet-green swallow) by Giselle Simons.

Line drawings on pages 156 (Lodgepole pine), 157 (Subalpine fir), 158 (Fairy slipper), 160 (Shooting star), 165 (Rocky Mountain bighorn sheep, Black bear), 166 (Coyote), 168 (Moose, Mule deer), 171 (American dipper), 173 (Golden eagle), and 175 (Red-tailed hawk) by Jasper Burns.

# Welcome to Rocky Mountain National Park

*S*now-covered peaks stand watch over lush valleys and shimmering alpine lakes, creating the perfect image of America's most dramatic and beautiful landscape—the majestic Rocky Mountains. Here, the pine- and fir-scented forests are deep, the air is crisp and pure, and the rugged mountain peaks reach up to grasp the deep blue sky. The views are simply spectacular.

Rocky Mountain National Park—Rocky to its friends—is unique, not only because of its breathtaking scenery, but also because of its diverse terrain, caused in large part by the extremes of elevation it encompasses. There are the ponderosa pine and juniper forests at its relatively low altitudes; there are the stands of Engelmann spruce and subalpine fir amid meadows of wildflowers; and as one moves onward and upward into the treeless alpine tundra, there is a bleak, rocky world very similar to the Arctic.

A prime wildlife-viewing area, the park is home not only to its famous elk, which often congregate in herds in meadows and on mountainsides, but also to mule deer, beavers, coyotes, river otters, moose, bighorn sheep, and an abundance of songbirds. Small mammals, such as chipmunks and squirrels, are almost always skittering about the viewpoints along Trail Ridge Road, as well as the campgrounds and picnic areas, where they have learned that sloppy humans tend to leave bits of food.

Trail Ridge Road, which cuts west through the middle of the park from Estes Park, then south down the park's western boundary to the community of Grand Lake, is one of America's great alpine highways. Consistently rated among the most scenic highways in America, Trail Ridge Road was designated an All-American Road in 1996, one of the first six in the nation. Climbing to 12,183 feet near Fall River Pass, it is the highest continuous paved highway in the United States. The road is usually open from Memorial Day to mid-October, depending on snowfall. The 48-mile scenic drive from Estes Park to Grand Lake takes about 3 hours, allowing for stops at some of its numerous scenic viewpoints. Exhibits at the Alpine Visitor Center at Fall River Pass, 11,796 feet above sea level, explain life on the alpine tundra.

Fall River Road and what is now called Old Fall River Road, the original park road, lead from Estes Park to Fall River Pass via Horseshoe Park. West of the Endovalley picnic area, the road is one-way uphill, and closed to trailers and motor homes. As you negotiate its gravelly switchbacks, you get a clear idea of what early auto travel was like in the West. This road, too, is closed in winter.

One of the few paved roads in the Rockies that leads into a high mountain basin is Bear Lake Road, which is kept open year-round, with occasional half-day closings to clear snow. Numerous trails converge at Bear Lake, southwest of the Beaver Meadows Visitor Center via Moraine Park.

One particularly inviting aspect of Rocky Mountain National Park is that it can be experienced in a variety of ways, and on many levels. While the adventurers savor the challenging hiking trails and backcountry routes, the curious will relish the unique opportunity to examine millions of years of geologic history, as well as the chance to see rare plant and animal species. Meanwhile, those with an artistic bent might totally ignore the recreational and educational aspects of the park and lose themselves in its beauty. Those new to the mountains may simply want to step back and let the total experience wash over them, finding a sense of peace in the serenity and natural wilderness of the park.

In searching for the essence of the park's natural world—its mountains, lakes, rivers, plants, and animals—you'll find well-developed and well-maintained trail systems, overlooks offering panoramic vistas, scenic drives and guided tours, interpretive displays, museum programs, and knowledgeable park rangers ready to help you make the most of your visit. At first it may seem overwhelming—you wonder, *How can I possibly see everything there is to be seen here?* Don't try. Forget about visiting Rocky as if it were an amusement park, racing from ride to ride; this park should be savored, embraced, and

## One Gutsy Lady!

Isabella Lucy Bird, an intrepid Englishwoman returning home from the Hawaiian Islands in the fall of 1873, spent about 3 months exploring what we now call the Front Range of the Rockies, on horseback and mostly by herself. Crossing into the interior of the continent by rail from California, she left the train at Cheyenne, Wyoming, and headed south into Colorado. Her goal, she wrote, was "a most romantic place called Estes Park, at a height of 7,500 feet."

She arrived in late September and observed, "Long's Peak, 14,700 feet high, dwarfs all the surrounding mountains." Then, 5 years after the first successful ascent of Longs Peak, Bird became the first woman to reach the top. "It was something at last to stand upon the storm-rent crown of this lonely sentinel of the Rocky Range. Uplifted above love and hate and storms of passion, calm amidst the eternal silences, fanned by zephyrs and bathed in living blue, peace rested for that one bright day on the Peak," she wrote to her sister.

Bird spent several weeks that autumn in a small cabin on Lake Estes. Nights were dark except for the brilliance of the stars, morning frosts were sharp, and water was carried from the lake. In late October, she embarked on a tour of Colorado's Front Range, riding a bay pony, "a little beauty, with legs of iron, fast, enduring, gentle, and wise," disregarding warnings of hostile American Indians and the threat of snow and cold. Undeterred, Bird headed south across the plains, staying in lodgings when available, but camping out under the stars at other times. She followed rivers and trails through Denver to Old Colorado City, located in present-day Colorado Springs. Turning once more toward the mountains, she passed through the rich red rocks known as the Garden of the Gods, and listened to tales of the healing powers of the springs of Manitou. Winding her way back north, she endured snow blindness and bitter cold, before again reaching Estes Park, and writing, "Nothing I have seen in Colorado compares with Estes Park."

In early December, Isabella Bird left Estes Park for the final time, returning to the train at Cheyenne and eventually home to afternoon tea, fine linens, and a warm, soft bed in England. And although she later traveled to Japan, India, Turkey, and China, she never again visited the land she had fondly called the Wild West.

explored, and the best way to do that is to move slowly. Take the time to ponder a sunrise as it illuminates Longs Peak, to sit quietly at the edge of a meadow while waiting for an elk or deer to emerge from the woods for its evening meal, and even, as the cliché goes, to stop and smell the flowers.

It's almost certain that you won't see every corner of the park, even on a long vacation of 2 or 3 weeks. Rocky is enormous and overpowering. It's difficult to look at these peaks and the harshness of the alpine tundra, and to refrain from thinking about the place of humanity, and to some extent our insignificance, in the scheme of things. Although this can be a difficult and time-consuming park to explore—ask anyone who has climbed Longs Peak—Rocky is also, on a different level, one of the West's most accessible national parks. This is due in large part to Trail Ridge Road and an excellent trail system, which offers a surprisingly large number of easy-to-moderate hikes that can be accomplished in a few hours or less. This enables the visitor to explore the park in fairly small, easily digestible bites, sampling one aspect, letting it settle, and then moving along for another taste.

## 1  A Look at Rocky Mountain National Park Today

Like all of America's national parks, Rocky is in a period of transition, as the National Park Service attempts to deal with the increasing number of visitors; the growth of nearby cities; the challenge of financing; and, probably the most important, the changes in philosophy in its role as a steward of America's best natural lands.

It's important to realize that when the National Park Service was young, in the early 20th century, it took its role of protecting national parks a bit too literally, at least when compared with today's understanding of the workings of nature. Back then, park managers sincerely believed that they should, in fact, manage every aspect of the parks, and they began fighting all fires, regardless of origin, and eliminating certain native animals so that others could flourish. Park service worker Jack Moomaw wrote about the errors 1920s park employees made in *Recollections of a Rocky Mountain Ranger* (Estes Park, CO: YMCA of the Rockies): "In those days, part

of a ranger's winter work was trapping all the so-called preda-
tory animals. Later we decided that all of the animals have
their rightful place in the scheme of things, and we protect
them all alike."

Today, the park service focuses most of its efforts on man-
aging the people who visit the parks, and, as much as possible,
on letting nature take care of the park itself. If the park service is playing God, it is doing so in its attempt to undo some
of the damage done to the park in the past. It is replacing
native grasses where they were destroyed by domestic grazing
by cattle and sheep, and planting native tree species in areas
where they had been eliminated by grazing, man-made fires,
or other actions directly attributable to human beings.

Although many of the environmental problems caused by
people take a while to become obvious, others can demand
attention very quickly. Such was the case on July 15, 1982,
when, at 5:30am, the Lawn Lake Dam failed. One of five
dams built prior to the establishment of the park, the Lawn
Lake Dam had doubled the size of the natural Lawn Lake, in
the Mummy Range located in the northern section of the
park.

When the privately owned 26-foot earthen dam was
breached, more than 200 million gallons of water—a 30-foot-
high wall—crashed down the Roaring River into the Fall
River drainage, ripping out trees, picking up boulders, and
digging into the mountainsides, before depositing debris in
Horseshoe Park and beyond. As the flood waters continued
their journey, they caused a smaller dam to fail, and eventually
made their way to downtown Estes Park, covering the community in water measuring up to 6 feet deep, plus mud, rocks,
sand, and trees. The water had traveled 12.5 miles in 3½
hours, killed three people in the park, and caused over $40
million in damage to the town of Estes Park. After the flood,
all the remaining private dams within the park were removed.

The park service also functions as the security force at
Rocky. Rangers at the park are carrying guns, and it's not for
protection from mountain lions and bears. No, park rangers
are a lot more concerned with human predators.

As Colorado grows, and people everywhere become more
mobile, Rocky Mountain National Park is finding that it has
more and more of what are considered urban problems: thefts,

vandalism, drug use, and assaults. Graffiti has marred rocks at Many Parks Curve, Moraine Park Campground, and other locations, and campers and sightseers are being warned to lock their vehicles and to refrain from leaving valuables at campsites.

In addition, it seems that some of the less-desirable residents of Colorado's Front Range, which contains more than half of the state's population and is within a few hours' drive of the park, have discovered that the remoteness of the park makes it a good hideout. Park rangers say that of the three dozen or so arrests made each year, about half are on warrants from Front Range communities.

This is not to say that the park is not safe. Statistically, it is still safer to visit a national park than to go most other places; but times change, and no matter how much we would like it otherwise, we cannot escape the problems of so-called civilization.

## 2  The Best of Rocky Mountain National Park

From its rocky peaks to its deep forests and cold, clear lakes, Rocky Mountain National Park is an enchanting world of spectacular scenic wonders, and a magnificent outdoor playground. In fact, the only real problem here is choosing which trails to hike, at which vistas to stop, what programs to attend, where to stay, and where to eat. Because there are so many options, planning a trip to the park can be a bewildering experience. To give you a head start on your planning, we've assembled a list of the very best that this park and the surrounding areas have to offer.

### THE BEST EASY HIKES & WALKS

- **Copeland Falls Trail:** There's a lot of wonderful scenery packed into this easy walk, only 0.6 miles round-trip, which follows a creek past wildflowers, aspens, stands of large fir and spruce, and Rocky Mountain maples to a picturesque little waterfall. See chapter 4.
- **Coyote Valley Nature Trail:** Following the Colorado River through the Kawuneeche Valley, this 1-mile loop trail offers excellent opportunities to see wildlife and to explore a lodgepole pine forest. See chapter 4.

- **Sprague Lake Nature Trail:** Not only does this easy 0.5-mile loop trail provide great views of glaciers and several of the park's most scenic mountains, but when the water is calm and the light is right, you get a double view—the dramatic skyline is reflected in the lake. See chapter 4.

## THE BEST SHORT DAY HIKES

- **Emerald Lake Trail:** Hike less than 4 miles round-trip and you can see three pretty lakes and the surrounding mountains and walk through a forest of limber and lodgepole pines and fir trees that has meadows of wildflowers in summer. Rated easy to moderate. See chapter 4.
- **Ouzel Falls Trail:** One of the most picturesque waterfalls in a park that has many picturesque waterfalls, Ouzel Falls is also a good spot to see the water ouzel (also known as the American dipper), a bird that collects its dinner by darting into the water. About 5.5 miles round-trip, this moderate hike passes several other falls and crosses a creek along the way. See chapter 4.
- **The Loch Trail:** Alternating between forests and open slopes, this 5.4-mile round-trip moderately rated hike offers good close-up views of wildflowers, as well as panoramic views of nearby peaks, glaciers, and the dramatic three-tiered Timberline Falls. See chapter 4.
- **Lake Haiyaha Trail:** Perhaps this should be called Many Lakes Trail, since not only do you see Lake Haiyaha (Hi-*yah*-hah), but this 4.2-mile round-trip moderate hike also offers views of Dream, Nymph, Bear, Mills, and Sprague lakes, plus a pond or two. The views of Longs Peak are also pretty spectacular. See chapter 4.

## THE BEST LONG DAY HIKES

- **Chasm Lake Trail:** Some of the best views in the park are your reward for sweating your way up a fairly steep slope past the tree line on this difficult 8.4-mile round-trip hike. You'll see wildflowers, wildlife, a waterfall, a picturesque lake, and a perfect view of Longs Peak. See chapter 4.
- **Fern Lake Trail:** Early fall is the best time to hike this 7.6-mile round-trip moderate trail, when the aspen, Rocky Mountain maple, and cottonwoods turn the forest into a kaleidoscope of colors. On the way to Fern Lake, with the Little Matterhorn peak rising majestically above it, you'll see wildflowers, a waterfall, and several stone monoliths. See chapter 4.

- **Onahu Creek/Green Mountain Loop Trail:** One of the best "deep forest" trails, this moderate 7-mile loop follows several creeks through stands of aspen, fir, spruce, and lodgepole pine, before traveling the edge of a colorful meadow of wildflowers. See chapter 4.

## THE BEST OVERNIGHT HIKES

- **East Longs Peak Trail:** Although this hike is not for everyone, experienced mountaineers in good physical shape will find this to be one of the park's most challenging and rewarding treks. There are spectacular views practically in all directions when looking straight down from atop 14,255-foot Longs Peak, Rocky Mountain National Park's highest point. Although the hike can be accomplished in one very long day, it's far more enjoyable to make it a 2-day excursion. See chapter 4.

- **Over the Continental Divide:** Separated by the Continental Divide, the park's west side is somewhat different from the east side, in terrain, climate, and even flora and fauna. To see these two sides of the park by foot involves a difficult 15-mile hike of two or more days, but you'll see a vast variety of scenery and wildlife. Take the North Inlet Trail near Grand Lake, through the subalpine region into the alpine tundra, past fields of wildflowers and spectacular peaks, to Flattop Mountain, on the Continental Divide. Here you change trails, heading down out of the tundra, past views of pretty lakes and several usually snowcapped peaks, to Bear Lake, on the park's east side. See chapter 4.

## THE BEST PLACES TO SEE WILDLIFE

- **Trail Ridge Road:** It's almost unbelievable how easy it is to see wildlife while driving along Trail Ridge Road. In fact, if you don't see birds and at least some squirrels and other small mammals, then you must have slept through the ride. In addition to the numerous squirrels and chipmunks, look for deer and elk in the meadows along the road, and yellow-bellied marmots and pikas at the higher elevations. Watch for the numerous birds, such as mountain bluebirds, Steller's jays, Clark's nutcrackers, prairie falcons, and golden eagles. See chapter 3.

- **Coyote Valley Nature Trail:** This easy walk in the Kawuneeche Valley offers a chance at glimpsing a variety of wildlife, including elk, moose, coyotes, weasels, porcupines, and squirrels. See chapter 4.

- **Moraine Park Campground:** Both in the campground and along the road leading to it from Bear Lake Road, watch for elk, deer, and smaller mammals such as chipmunks and squirrels. See chapter 5.

## THE BEST LOCATION FOR WINTER SPORTS

- **Wild Basin Area:** In the southeast corner of the park, Wild Basin offers great cross-country skiing. Start on the last mile of the entry road, which is closed to motor vehicles in winter. The road leads to the trailhead for the wonderful Ouzel Falls Trail, where you'll usually see a wide variety of birds. See chapter 4.

## THE BEST RANGER/OUTFITTER-LED ACTIVITIES

- **A Moonlight Snowshoe Hike:** A still, moonlit evening in January or February is perfect for a snowshoe hike with a ranger, who may discuss the adaptation of the park's animals to the long winters, and the wildlife you are likely to see at night. Or maybe your group will quietly absorb the scenery as moonlight glistens on fields of snow, mountains stand tall against the night sky, and a chorus of coyotes breaks the stillness. See chapter 3.

- **Rocky Mountain Nature Association Seminars:** Although topics for these half-, full-, and multiday programs vary, you can bet that the instructors will be knowledgeable and interesting. Most of the seminars take place in the park and involve at least a little walking or hiking. If offered during your visit, consider participating in the program on Wild Edible and Useful Plants, which travels to various sites in the park to find edible, medicinal, and even poisonous plants. See chapter 4.

- **A Longs Peak Climb with Colorado Mountain School:** We prefer doing most things in the park on our own, but attempting a climb up ice-covered rock to the park's tallest peak isn't one of them. We recommend going with the experts at this park-sanctioned school. See chapter 4.

## THE BEST ACTIVITIES FOR KIDS

- **Ranger-Led Hike to the Beaver Ponds:** Beavers are fun animals to watch, but it's often hard to find them on your own. Rangers lead a special kids' hike to the park's beaver ponds to show the kids where the beavers live and how they build their dams. If you're lucky, a beaver may make an appearance. See chapter 3.

- **Bear Lake:** This easy nature walk around Bear Lake is a good opportunity for parents (using the park's trail-guide booklet) to talk about Rocky's plants and animals with their children. It's also a good opportunity for kids to see animals such as snow-shoe hares and chipmunks, and by peering down into the lake's water, they may even catch a glimpse of the Colorado state fish—the greenback cutthroat trout. See chapter 4.

## THE BEST VIEWPOINTS

- **Many Parks Curve:** This stop along Trail Ridge Road offers splendid views of numerous mountains and the valleys between them. It is also a good spot to see innumerable birds and small, begging squirrels and chipmunks (which you should never feed!). See chapter 3.
- **Rock Cut:** At 12,110 feet, this is one of the highest points along Trail Ridge Road, and it's a good stop for those who want to experience the harsh alpine tundra while staying within a few feet of the warmth and comfort of their cars. For an even better look, walk the relatively easy 0.5-mile loop of the Tundra World Nature Trail, where exhibits identify the flora and fauna of the tundra and explain why you wouldn't want to live here year-round. See chapter 3.

## THE BEST HISTORIC SITES

- **Never Summer Ranch:** This was rugged country in the early 20th century—it still is, of course—and conditions for tourists were primitive, to say the least. At this ranch, which has been preserved by the park service, you'll see kitchens, a taxidermy shop, and the primitive bunkhouses and other facilities that were rented out to early park visitors, and be grateful that things have changed. See chapter 3.
- **Old Fall River Road:** The national park's original dirt road is still in use and little changed from its opening in 1920. It gives today's motorists an idea of what it was like to drive into the park some 80 years ago. See chapter 3.
- **Lulu City:** Although there isn't a great deal to see here except some cabin ruins and rusty pieces of mining equipment, it can be fascinating to imagine what Lulu City was like more than 100 years ago, when this silver boomtown had a hotel, two saw mills, a variety of shops, and even a small red-light district. See chapters 3 and 4.

## THE BEST NATIONAL PARK & NATIONAL FOREST CAMPGROUNDS

- **Moraine Park Campground:** Although this is the park's biggest campground, with almost 250 sites, an abundance of ponderosa pines and good design give it a much smaller feel. Also, we like a campground where elk and deer think they own the place. See chapter 5.
- **Longs Peak Campground:** It's rare to find a drive-in campground anywhere that permits tent camping only, but this one does. And it is a welcome relief for tenters to know they won't be walled in by apartment-building–size motor homes and trailers. See chapter 5.
- **Olive Ridge Campground:** This forest service campground just outside the southeast corner of the park offers a true forest camping experience, with plenty of trees, well-spaced sites, and good chances of seeing wildlife. See chapter 5.

## THE BEST FULL-SERVICE RV PARKS

- **Spruce Lake R.V. Park** (Estes Park; ☎ 970/586-2889): It's hard to call this camping—it's simply too refined. Open to RVs only (no ground tents), the carpeted bathhouses are among the cleanest and most luxurious we've seen anywhere, and with a stocked private fishing lake, miniature golf, and weekly ice-cream socials, it may be hard to find time for exploring the national park. See chapter 5.
- **Elk Creek Campground and RV Park** (Grand Lake; ☎ 800/355-2733): Close to the national park's west entrance, this commercial campground has tree-shaded, well-spaced sites that give it the feel of a national park or forest service campground, while also providing complete RV hookups and hot showers that will help you get a good night's sleep at the end of a busy day of hiking. See chapter 5.

## THE BEST ACTIVITIES OUTSIDE THE PARK

- **Bowen Gulch Interpretive Trail:** An easy walk leads to an old-growth spruce-fir forest, where there's a good chance of seeing wildlife, and a free brochure helps explain this unique ecosystem. See chapter 6.
- **The Cache la Poudre Wild and Scenic River:** It's hard to imagine a better way to spend a hot summer day than bouncing through the rapids on this wet-and-wild roller coaster, while

admiring the beautiful scenery surrounding Rocky Mountain
National Park. See chapter 6.

- **Enos Mills Homestead Cabin** (Estes Park; ☎ 970/
  586-4706): A prime supporter of the creation of Rocky
  Mountain National Park, Enos Mills may be less known
  than other prominent conservationists of his day, such
  as John Muir, but he was no less influential. A visit to
  his 1885 cabin takes you back to a much simpler time,
  and an informal talk with a member of the Mills family provides much insight into the character of this
  region 100 years ago. See chapter 6.

- **Lake Granby:** Catch a trout from either the shore or a rented
  boat. The fish are almost always biting at Lake Granby, which
  is stocked with rainbows and browns. See chapter 6.

## THE BEST NEARBY LODGING

- **Aspen Lodge at Estes Park** (Estes Park; ☎ 970/586-8133):
  Although not actually inside the national park, this huge log
  cabin certainly captures the park's atmosphere, and most rooms
  and cabins have a splendid view of Longs Peak. Trails from the
  resort's 82 acres lead directly into the park. See chapter 6.

- **Boulder Brook** (Estes Park; ☎ 800/238-0910): For luxurious
  accommodations in a beautiful mountain setting, it's hard to
  beat the Boulder Brook's suites, with fireplaces, whirlpool tubs
  or spas, views of the Fall River, and as much pampering as you
  can stand. See chapter 6.

- **Alpine Trail Ridge Inn** (Estes Park; ☎ 800/233-5023): An
  excellent choice for those on a budget, this moderately priced
  property offers a wide range of clean, comfortable accommodations and a great location—there's a path just outside the motel
  that leads to the national-park visitor center. An added plus is
  that the innkeepers are avid hikers who enjoy helping guests
  plan their park visits. See chapter 6.

- **Baldpate Inn** (Estes Park; ☎ 970/586-6151): This small inn
  is open only in summer and most rooms share bathrooms, but
  it has personality galore. There are handmade quilts,
  early–20th-century furnishings, and a large stone fireplace in
  the living room. It also offers an excellent soup-and-salad buffet dinner. See chapter 6.

- **Grand Lake Lodge** (Grand Lake; ☎ 970/627-3967): If you
  came to Rocky Mountain National Park for the scenery, this is

the perfect place to stay. The lodge bills itself as Colorado's "favorite front porch," and with views of Grand Lake and a backdrop of spectacular mountains, we can't argue with that assessment. See chapter 6.

- **Daven Haven Lodge** (Grand Lake; ☎ **970/627-8144**): As they say in the real estate business: location, location, location. This group of modern cabins is set among pine trees, about a mile from the lake, in a setting so peaceful and serene you may want to stay forever. But actually, one of our favorite aspects of the lodge is in the lobby—a wondrous collection of antique jukeboxes. See chapter 6.

## THE BEST NEARBY DINING

- **Andrea's of Estes** (Estes Park; ☎ **970/586-0886**): Fine dining with an emphasis on German cuisine and wild game makes Andrea's a good lunch or dinner choice, but the views of the national park from its rooftop deck make it a must-do experience. See chapter 6.

- **Molly B** (Estes Park; ☎ **970/586-2766**): Breakfast at Molly B is the perfect way to prepare for a day of serious hiking, and you won't have to worry about going away hungry. Try one of the spicy specialties or opt for a conservative American basic such as bacon and eggs. See chapter 6.

- **The Dunraven Inn** (Estes Park; ☎ **970/586-6409**): This dinner-only fine-dining restaurant is the place to go to celebrate a special occasion or perhaps to reward yourself for finally making it to the top of Longs Peak. The Dunraven serves a variety of Italian specialties and is memorably decorated with numerous images of the *Mona Lisa,* including one sporting a mustache. See chapter 6.

- **E.G.'s Garden Grill** (Grand Lake; ☎ **970/627-8404**): Ask any resident of Grand Lake where to go for lunch or dinner, and the response will likely be, "E.G.'s." The menu offers innovative items such as catfish with jalapeño tartar sauce, something one doesn't expect to find in a small Colorado mountain town. See chapter 6.

# 2

# Planning Your Trip

*I*n the not-too-distant past, planning a visit to a national park—particularly one in the western United States—involved little more than choosing a date and packing the car. The availability of a campsite was a given, and you could generally wait until you arrived to decide exactly what you wanted to do. Those days are over. Today, a wise traveler should invest a bit of time doing research before arriving at a park. Before setting out for your destination, you should read guidebooks such as this one, contact park offices for maps and current information, check out lodging and camping choices, and make reservations. A smart planner will also research restaurant, shopping, and side-trip possibilities.

There are several reasons for this need for early preparation. As more people—from this country and others—discover the parks, crowds there are increasing, and it's becoming much harder to find campsites, lodging, and even parking. To combat this problem, it's best to decide what you want to do at the park ahead of time and then to try to schedule your visit for a less-crowded time that best suits those activities. For instance, as you'll discover in the following chapters, guided horseback rides are offered only during the warmer months, the busiest times at Rocky Mountain National Park. If horseback riding is something you want to do but you'd prefer to avoid the masses, schedule your trip for late spring or early fall—the so-called shoulder seasons—when the stables are open, but before the summer hordes arrive or after they have departed.

Another good reason for advance planning is that you don't want to waste precious vacation time searching for a motel or campsite vacancy. Luckily, there are far more lodging and dining choices in and around the national parks than there were even 10 or 20 years ago. Back then we were happy if we found a restaurant that was clean and served basic American food. Today the choices are phenomenal, and dining out has

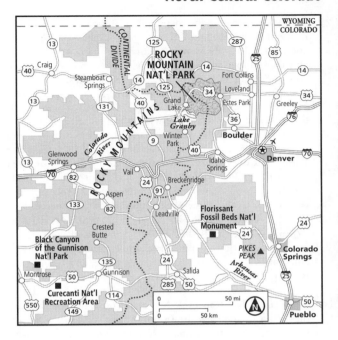

evolved from simply filling the stomach into an important part of the national park vacation experience.

Don't dread the trip research—like the anticipation of, and preparation for, a birthday party, Christmas, or another special event, planning a vacation to a national park can be loads of fun.

## 1 Getting Started: Information & Reservations

**Rocky Mountain National Park** will send you a free park brochure, map, and other information on the activities available at the park. To get these items, you can contact the Superintendent, Rocky Mountain National Park, Estes Park, CO 80517-8397 (☎ **970/586-1206**). The park's Web site is www.nps.gov/romo.

Another good source of information is the nonprofit **Rocky Mountain Nature Association** (☎ **800/816-7662** or 970/586-0108; www.rmna.org/bookstore). The association

sells a number of park maps, guides, books, and videos—
many in both VHS and PAL formats. Members of the association
get a 15% discount on purchases at Rocky Mountain
and many other national parks. Membership has an annual
cost of $15 for individuals and $25 for families. Videos and
interactive CD-ROMs are also available from **Interpark,**
1540 E. MacArthur St., Cortez, CO 81321 (☎ **800/
687-5967** or 970/565-7453; www.petroglyphtrail.com).

Information on the national park, as well as activities and
facilities just outside the park, can be obtained from the **Estes
Park Chamber Resort Association,** 500 Big Thompson Ave.,
Estes Park, CO 80517 (☎ **800/44-ESTES** or 970/586-4431;
fax 970/586-6336; www.estesparkresort.com). You can also
contact the **Grand Lake Area Chamber of Commerce,** P.O.
Box 57, Grand Lake, CO 80447 (☎ **800/531-1019** or
970/627-3372; fax 970/627-8007; www.grandlakechamber.
com; e-mail: glinfo@grandlakechamber.com). Estes Park is
adjacent to the national park's east entrance, and Grand Lake
is just outside the west entrance.

The national park is practically surrounded by national-
forest lands. The **Roosevelt National Forest** borders the park
on the north and east, the **Indian Peaks Wilderness Area** is
to the south, and the **Arapaho National Forest and Arapaho
National Recreation Area** lie along the west side of the park.
To obtain information on camping, hiking, mountain biking,
fishing, cross-country skiing, snowshoeing, and numerous
other activities in the national forests, contact the **Forest Service Information Center,** 1311 S. College Ave., Fort Collins,
CO 80524 (☎ **970/498-2770**), and the Arapaho National
Forest's **Sulphur Ranger District Office,** P.O. Box 10, Granby,
CO 80446 (☎ **970/887-4100**). In Estes Park, a **Forest Service Information Center** is located at 161 Second St.
(☎ **970/586-3440**); it's open daily in summer and has limited
hours for several days a week in winter. The U.S. Forest Service's **Rocky Mountain Region office,** P.O. Box 25127,
Lakewood, CO 80225 (☎ **303/236-9431**), can also provide
you with information. The U.S. Forest Service Web site for
this region is www.fs.fed.us/r2.

Web surfers will find detailed information about hiking,
fishing, biking, water sports, and other activities on Colorado's public lands, including Rocky Mountain National Park,

in the Colorado section of **GORP** (Great Outdoor Recreation Page; **www.gorp.com**), which has links to other related sites. We've also found some good information at **www.altrec.com/magazine** and its sister site, **www.greatoutdoors.com**.

Camping reservations are accepted for two of the park's campgrounds during the summer. (For more information, see chapter 5.) Lodging reservations are recommended in both Estes Park and Grand Lake, especially in July and August. (For more information, see chapter 6.) Those planning horseback trips or other excursions with local outfitters will want to make reservations as early as possible. (For more information, see chapter 4.)

**USEFUL PUBLICATIONS/BOOKS/VIDEOS**    Although we have tried to pack as much information as possible into this book, you may want some additional details or another perspective before your trip. The Rocky Mountain Nature Association (see "Getting Started: Information & Reservations," earlier in this chapter) is an excellent information source, providing mail orders as well as operating the bookshops at the park. Another good source for regional books and advice on what books might be of interest to you is **Macdonald Book Shop,** 152 E. Elkhorn Ave. (P.O. Box 900), Estes Park, CO 80517 (☎ **970/586-3450;** www.macdonaldbookshop.com; e-mail: macdonaldbooks@aol.com).

An excellent guidebook, *Hiking Rocky Mountain National Park* (Old Saybrook, CT: The Globe Pequot Press), by Kent and Donna Dannen, gives detailed trail descriptions; and the informative *Rocky Mountain National Park Road Guide* (Jackson Hole, WY: Free Wheeling Travel Guides), by Thomas Schmidt, provides thumbnail sketches of virtually everything you'll see along the park's roadways. Those who plan to do serious backpacking may want to consider buying *U.S. Geological Survey* topographic maps or the accurate and easy-to-follow *Trails Illustrated* map of the park.

History buffs looking for an 1870s perspective of the land that would become Rocky Mountain National Park should try the fascinating first-person narrative *A Lady's Life in the Rocky Mountains* (Norman, Okla.: University of Oklahoma Press), by Isabella Bird. For a historical view starting in the 1920s, you may want a copy of *Recollections of a Rocky Mountain Ranger* (Estes Park, CO: YMCA of the Rockies), by Jack C. Moomaw. A thorough and well-researched history of the park is presented in ***Rocky Mountain National Park: A History*** (Niwot, CO: University Press of Colorado), by C. W. Buchholtz.

Among available videos, we recommend ***Rocky Mountain National Park,*** which presents a colorful glimpse of the park's wondrous scenery and is available from Interpark (see "Getting Started: Information & Reservations," earlier in this chapter).

## 2  When to Go

Even though the park is open year-round, **Trail Ridge Road,** the park's main east-west thoroughfare, is always closed in winter. It's safe to assume that you will not be able to drive clear across the park from mid-October until Memorial Day, and even in summer it's quite possible that the road will be closed for hours, or even a day or more, by snow.

That's not to say that intrepid travelers can't enjoy the park in winter. All of the park's entrances are open, trails are open to snowshoers and cross-country skiers, and the roads to a number of good viewpoints and trailheads are plowed. There are even a few accessible hiking trails. Skiers with the proper skills and equipment can cross-country ski into the high country, but they need to keep aware of storm and avalanche dangers, and should always check with rangers before setting out. Permits are required for all overnight trips into the backcountry (see "Permits You Can Obtain in Advance," below).

**AVOIDING THE CROWDS**    The park is fully accessible for less than half the year, so that's when most people visit. The very busiest time is from mid-June to mid-August—essentially during school vacation—so going just before or just after that period is best. Because most people explore the park between 10am and 4pm, you can avoid most of the crowds by going to viewpoints and trails early or late in the day. The light's better for photographs at those times, and you're more apt to see wildlife then, anyway.

Winter is gaining in popularity, even though you can't drive the entire Trail Ridge Road. Although the park can be bitterly cold, this is the quietest time, when you'll most likely see plenty of elk, moose, and other large animals. In addition, the views of stately evergreens on snow-covered mountains set against a sky of azure blue are unforgettable.

Regardless of when you visit, the best way to avoid crowds is to simply walk away from them on one of the numerous trails.

**Park Visitors 1999**

| | |
|---|---|
| January | 72,510 |
| February | 86,387 |
| March | 96,280 |
| April | 61,024 |
| May | 199,799 |
| June | 485,377 |
| July | 777,092 |
| August | 667,173 |
| September | 491,288 |
| October | 238,547 |
| November | 102,976 |
| December | 86,704 |
| **Total** | 3,366,253 |

**CLIMATE & WEATHER**   A key factor that will affect your trip to the park in any season is weather. Because of the park's high elevation and its extreme range of elevations, you'll find that temperatures and other weather conditions will vary greatly. Essentially, the higher into the mountains you go, the cooler and wetter it gets. Rangers say that for every 1,000 feet in elevation gain, you can expect a climate change equivalent to that of traveling 600 miles north, and an accompanying temperature drop of 3°F.

The tree line in the park—the elevation at which trees can no longer grow—varies somewhat but is generally set at about 11,500 feet. Also complicating the weather picture is the Continental Divide, which runs northwest to southeast through the park. It accounts for markedly different weather patterns—one on the east side near Estes Park and the other on the west side in the Grand Lake area. Usually the east side is somewhat drier and warmer than the west side.

Particularly at the higher elevations, windchill factors can be extreme. Hypothermia can be a problem at any time, even in summer, when afternoon thunderstorms occur without warning, causing temperatures to drop dramatically and suddenly. Winds of 200 miles per hour are possible in the higher mountain areas at any time of year, and wind speeds of 150 miles per hour have been recorded along Trail Ridge Road.

In summer, temperatures typically climb into the 70s and low 80s during the day and drop into the 40s and even 30s at night. July is the warmest month and usually sees an inch or more of rain, whereas August is the wettest month of the year, with about 2 inches of rain. Afternoon thunderstorms occur throughout the summer and pose a danger to people on unprotected ridges and in other open places.

Winters usually see high temperatures in the 20s and 30s and lows from 10° below zero to 20° above. January is the coldest month, although February may feel colder because of gusty winds that seem to cut right through you. November and December usually have only light snow, but the amount of snowfall increases through January, February, and March. Spring and fall temperatures can vary greatly, from pleasantly warm to bitterly cold and snowy. For this reason, spring and fall are when you need to be the most flexible and to adjust your itinerary to suit current conditions.

**SEASONAL ACTIVITIES**    Most of the ranger-led activities, such as amphitheater programs and guided hikes and walks, occur only during the summer, although a few are scheduled year-round. Some, such as guided snowshoe hikes and cross-country ski tours, obviously take place only when there's snow on the ground. (See chapter 3 for more details.)

Late June is usually the best time to see **wildflowers,** although Colorado columbine and some other flowers continue blooming through August. The **elk rutting** season from September to mid-October brings hundreds of elk to the lower elevations, where you can often hear the macho bulls bugle and can watch them try to keep other bulls from muscling in on their chosen females. This is also a particularly scenic time, when the aspen trees turn a brilliant gold, producing a delightful contrast with the deep greens of the fir and spruce trees.

## What Should I Take?

In packing for your trip, you'll want to be prepared for all your favorite activities, of course, but also keep in mind that this is a land of extremes, with an often unforgiving climate and terrain. Those planning to hike or bike should take more drinking-water containers than they think they'll need—experts recommend at least 1 gallon of water per person per day on the trail—as well as good-quality sunblock, hats and other protective clothing, and sunglasses with ultraviolet protection.

Summer visitors will want to carry rain gear for the typical afternoon thunderstorms, and jackets or sweaters for cool evenings and the biting winds that can appear at any time. We can't emphasize too strongly that warm clothing will very likely be needed at least once or twice during your visit, even at the height of summer. Winter visitors will want not only warm parkas and hats, but lighter clothing as well—the bright sun at midday, even in the high mountains, can make it feel almost like June.

Take a first-aid kit, of course, and make sure it contains tweezers—very useful for removing ticks and cactus spines. Hikers will appreciate having a walking stick, and those carrying cameras may want to consider using one that can double as a monopod. Binoculars are also a very welcome accessory.

There are also a number of seasonal activities that take place just outside the park in the communities of Estes Park and Grand Lake. (For more details, see chapter 6.)

## 3 Permits You Can Obtain in Advance

Day use of the park requires only the payment of the admission fees discussed in chapter 3. Permits, however, are required for all overnight backcountry trips; backcountry campsites can be reserved beginning on March 1 of each year. There is a $15 administrative fee charged for permits issued from May through October, but there is no charge at other times. Contact the park's **Backcountry Office** (☎ **970/586-1242**). (See "Exploring the Backcountry," in chapter 4, for more details.)

Advance reservations can be made with the **National Park Reservations Service** (☎ **800/365-2267** or 301/722-1257;

http://reservations.nps.gov), or make reservations through the park's Web site (www.nps.gov/romo) for summer camping at two of the park's campgrounds. (See chapter 5 for more information on campground reservations.)

## 4 Getting There

**BY PLANE**   Visitors arriving by plane will usually fly into **Denver International Airport** (☎ **800/247-2336** or 303/342-2000), which is about 90 miles southeast of the east entrances to the park. Airlines serving Denver include **Air Canada** (☎ 888/247-2262; www.aircanada.ca), **American** (☎ 800/433-7300; www.aa.com), **America West** (☎ 800/235-9292; www.americawest.com), **Continental** (☎ 800/525-0280; www.flycontinental.com), **Delta** (☎ 800/221-1212; www.delta.com), **Frontier** (☎ 800/432-1359; www.frontierairlines.com), **Korean Air** (☎ 800/438-5000; www.koreanair.com), **Martinair** (☎ 800/366-4655; www.martinair.com), **Mexicana** (☎ 800/531-7921; www.mexicana.com), **Midwest Express** (☎ 800/452-2022; www.midwestexpress.com), **Northwest** (☎ 800/225-2525; www.nwa.com), **Sun Country** (☎ 800/359-6786; www.suncountry.com), **TWA** (☎ 800/221-2000; www.twa.com), **United and United Express** (☎ 800/241-6522; www.ual.com), **US Airways** (☎ 800/428-4322; www.usair.com), and **Vanguard** (☎ 800/826-4827; www.flyvanguard.com).

**FLIGHTS FROM THE UNITED KINGDOM**   One daily nonstop direct flight between London and Denver is offered by **British Airways** (☎ **800/247-9297,** 0845/773-3377 in London; www.british-airways.com). Travelers from the United Kingdom can also take British Airways flights to other major U.S. cities and make connecting flights to Colorado.

From the Denver airport, travelers can either rent a car (see "By Car," below) or continue to Estes Park with **Estes Park Shuttle** (☎ **800/586-5009** or 970/586-5151; www.estesparkco.com).

**BY CAR**   Those using airlines or other public transportation to get to Colorado will likely arrive in Denver and will have to rent a car there. National rental agencies readily available include **Advantage** (☎ 800/777-5500; www.arac.com), **Alamo** (☎ 800/462-5266; www.goalamo.com), **Avis** (☎ 800/

# Colorado Driving Times & Distances

WYOMING  Cheyenne  NEBRASKA

Dinosaur Nat'l. Mon.  Steamboat Springs  ROCKY MTN. NAT'L. PARK  Fort Collins

129 **1:55**  94 **1:23**  93 **1:22**  47 **:41**

To Salt Lake City  Glenwood Springs  Denver  To Kansas City

285 **4:11**  155 **2:17**  76 **1:07**  449 **6:36**

89 **1:19**

Grand Junction

197 **2:54**  Colorado Springs  70 **1:02**  KANSAS

UTAH

Great Sand Dunes Nat'l Monument  42 **:37**  Pueblo

Mesa Verde Nat'l. Park  31 **:27**  122 **1:47**

Cortez  45 **:40**  149 **2:11**  Alamosa

39 **:34**  Durango  335 **4:56**

ARIZONA  Four Corners Monument  NEW MEXICO  To Albuquerque  OKLAHOMA

TEXAS

Note:
Lightface numbers *indicate driving distances in miles.*
**Boldface numbers** *indicate driving times.*
Driving time is based on an average speed of
68 miles per hour.

331-1212; www.avis.com), **Budget** (☎ 800/527-0700; www. budgetrentacar.com), **Dollar** (☎ 800/800-4000; www.dollarcar. com), **Enterprise** (☎ 800/325-8007; www.pickenterprise. com), **Hertz** (☎ 800/654-3131; www.hertz.com), **Kemwel Holiday Auto (KHA)** (☎ 800/576-1590; www.kemwel. com), **National** (☎ 888/227-7368; www.nationalcar.com), and **Thrifty** (☎ 800/847-4389; www.thrifty.com). Campers, travel trailers, and motor homes are available in Denver from **Cruise America** (☎ 800/327-7799; www.cruiseamerica. com); Harley-Davidson motorcycles can be rented in the Denver area at **Park Meadows Hog Rental** (☎ 303/ 799-0600; www.denverharleyrentals.com).

Most visitors enter the park from Estes Park, which is about 71 miles northwest of Denver, 34 miles northwest of Boulder, and 42 miles southwest of Fort Collins. The most direct route to Estes Park from Denver is via U.S. 36 through Boulder. At Estes Park, that highway joins U.S. 34, which runs up the Big

Thompson Canyon from I-25 and Loveland, and then continues through Rocky Mountain National Park to Grand Lake. An alternative scenic route from Denver to Estes Park is Colo. 7, the "Peak-to-Peak Scenic Byway" that transits Central City (Colo. 119), Nederland (Colo. 72), and Allenspark (Colo. 7) under different designations.

Those who want to enter the national park from the west can take U.S. 40 north from I-70 Exit 232, over the 11,307-foot Berthoud Pass, through Winter Park and Tabernash to Granby, and then follow U.S. 34 north to the village of Grand Lake and then on into the park. The distance from I-70 to the park entrance along this route is about 67 miles.

It's about 48 miles between the gateway cities of Estes Park and Grand Lake if you drive through the park on Trail Ridge Road, but this road is usually open only from late May to mid-October, and it can be closed by snow for hours, or even days, at any time. When Trail Ridge Road is closed, the shortest way to get from one side of the park to the other is to drive a big circle around the south side of the park, a scenic trip which covers 143 miles and takes about 3 hours.

From the Beaver Meadows Entrance Station on the east side of the national park, take U.S. 36 to Estes Park and go south on Colo. 7 for 14 miles through Allenspark to Colo. 72. Turn right (south) and continue 23 miles to Colo. 119, where you turn right (south) for 24 miles to U.S. 6. Head west on U.S. 6 for 3 miles, and then get on I-70 west for 12 miles to Exit 232, U.S. 40. Follow U.S. 40 for 52 miles north over Berthoud Pass and through Winter Park, Fraser (the self-proclaimed "icebox of the nation" at 8,574 ft. elevation), Tabernash, and Granby. Just north of Granby, turn right (east) onto U.S. 34 for 15 miles, skirting the western shores of Lake Granby and Shadow Mountain Lake, and continue past the turnoff to the community of Grand Lake and its namesake lake to the national park's western entrance.

## 5  Tips for RVers & Tenters

One of the best ways to explore Rocky Mountain National Park, especially in the warmer months, is in an RV (a motor home, truck camper, or camper trailer), or in a car or truck while spending your nights in a tent—provided you don't mind roughing it a bit.

Because early morning and early evening are often the best times to be in the park, and because there are no lodging facilities within the park's boundaries, camping at one of the park campgrounds will allow you to conveniently explore the park at these times. It will also give you the inexplicable feeling of contentment that comes from waking to the sound of birds singing and the sight of furry little creatures scurrying about outside your door; you're living the national-park experience rather than just visiting it as if it were an amusement park.

There are disadvantages, of course. Tents, small trailers, and campers can be cramped, and even the most luxurious motor homes and trailers provide somewhat close quarters. Facilities in national-park campgrounds are limited, although they are being upgraded to the point where camping purists are starting to complain. Even in most commercial campgrounds the facilities are less than what you'd expect in moderately priced hotels; and if you prepare your own meals you miss the opportunity to experience the local cuisine. But, all this aside, camping is just plain fun—especially in a setting as spectacularly beautiful as Rocky Mountain National Park.

Tenters who want to avoid the walled-in sensation, exhaust fumes, and noise of being surrounded by huge motor homes and trailers should consider Longs Peak Campground, which is open to tent camping only. Tenters should make sure that they have warm sleeping bags and extra clothing—nights are cold, even in summer. It is also **extremely important** that they bring airtight food containers that can be stored in car trunks or hung from trees in the backcountry. This will help avoid unwelcome visits from black bears and other wildlife.

There are also a few things that RVers should know. Old Fall River Road, a one-way uphill dirt route, is closed to all trailers, and motor homes over 25 feet long. Also, keep in mind that parking is limited in most sections of the park, especially for motor homes and other large vehicles. Most people, however, drive on park roads between 10am and 4pm, so the solution is to head out on the scenic drives either early or late in the day, when there's less traffic.

## Renting an RV for Your National Park Trek

If you own an RV, you're all set for a trip to Rocky Mountain National Park, but if you don't, you might want to consider renting one. In fact, a study by two Canadian anthropologists has concluded that compared to those in the general population, those who travel in RVs are happier, healthier, and have a greater sense of community.

First, let's get one thing straight: You probably won't save a lot of money. It is possible to travel fairly cheaply if you limit your equipment to a tent, a pop-up–tent trailer, or a small pick-up truck camper—but renting a motor home will probably end up costing almost as much as driving a compact car, staying in moderately priced motels, and eating in family-style restaurants and cafes. That's because motor homes will go only one-third as far on a gallon of gas as compact cars will, and they're fairly expensive to rent (generally between $1,000 and $1,200 per week in midsummer, when rates are highest).

But carrying your house with you, like a turtle, gives you the opportunity to stay in the national park campgrounds, which many park visitors believe is one of the highlights of their trips; it lets you stop for meals anytime and anywhere you choose; and it means you won't have to worry about sleeping on a lumpy pillow. An added benefit is that you won't spend time searching for a rest room—almost all RVs have some sort of bathroom facilities, ranging from a full bath with a tub/shower combination to a porta-potty stored under a seat.

RVs come in seemingly unlimited varieties, shapes, and sizes, and for the first-timer the choices can be both confusing and intimidating. We suggest that for a national-park vacation, especially a trip to a mountainous park such as Rocky Mountain, you choose the smallest RV you can find that still has the facilities you want. While practically every RV will have a toilet of some kind and a two-burner gas stove, smaller units often lack showers and ovens, and the smallest pop-up trailers and pickup campers often have iceboxes instead of refrigerators, which we consider false economy.

A trailer is advantageous in that it can be left in the campground while you go off exploring, and is an especially good choice if you'll be staying in one campsite for at least several days. However, we find trailers inconvenient when we're changing campsites every night because of the time needed for hitching and unhitching. Traditional hard-sided trailers are heavy and you'll need a large tow vehicle, probably a pickup truck or SUV. Pop-up–tent trailers are lightweight and easy to tow, but require extra time to set up and take down at each campsite. Another disadvantage to trailers is that you'll have a fairly long and hard-to-park unit when the trailer is being towed.

A motor home offers the most space, often a nice shower, a three- or four-burner stove with oven, a refrigerator with small freezer, and sometimes extras like coffeemakers, blenders, televisions, and music systems. But motor homes, especially the larger ones, require a lot of room to park, and you're likely to discover that you're passing by some scenic overlooks simply because there isn't enough space to accommodate your rig. Campsites are often too short for long motor homes, and there's one road at Rocky where motor homes over 25 feet long aren't permitted.

Our choice for a camping trip to Rocky, as well as most other national parks, is either a van camper or a pickup-truck camper. A van camper, often called a Class B camper, is essentially a full-size van with an extended roof, sleeping from two to four people, with a two- or three-burner stove, small refrigerator, sink, toilet, and sometimes a small shower. Pickup-truck campers also usually sleep up to four people and have basically the same equipment as van campers. The downside to both of these is that they have fairly limited storage capacity.

A packet of free information, including rental sources, RV shows, and a brochure titled *Go RVing: Everything You Need to Know to Get Started* is available from the **Recreational Vehicle Industry Association,** P.O. Box 2999, Dept. P, Reston, VA 20195 (☎ **888/GO-RVing;** www.rvia.org or www.gorving. com). The organization also offers a free 18-minute video on RV rental, shopping, and travel tips. You can obtain more information on renting an RV from the **Recreational Vehicle Rental Association's** Web site, **www.rvra.org**. For rental sources near the park, see "Getting There," above.

If you'll be traveling in the park in your RV and want to make it obvious that your campsite is occupied, carry something worthless to leave in it, such as a cardboard box with "Site Taken" clearly written on it. You can usually find a rock to weight it down.

Because some of the national-park campsites are not level, savvy RVers carry four or five short boards, or leveling blocks, that can be placed under the RV's wheels. You can buy small, inexpensive levels at RV and hardware stores, and you'll discover that not only will you sleep better if your rig is level, but your food won't slide off the table and the refrigerator will run more efficiently.

Once you've got an RV or tent, you'll need a place to put it, of course. See chapter 5 for information on camping in and around Rocky Mountain National Park. Those seeking information on campgrounds in other parts of the state can contact the **Colorado Agency of Camping, Cabins, & Lodges,** 5101 Pennsylvania Ave., Boulder, CO 80303-2799 (☎ **888/ 222-4641** or 303/499-9343; fax 303/499-9333; www. coloradodirectory.com). The agency publishes a free annual booklet describing commercial campgrounds, cabin facilities, bed-and-breakfast inns, and resorts throughout the state. A free copy of *Colorado State Parks,* a brochure with details on the state's 40-plus parks, is available from state park offices, 1313 Sherman St., no. 618, Denver, CO 80203 (☎ **303/ 866-3437;** www.coloradoparks.org).

There are close to 30 KOA franchise campgrounds in Colorado, which all offer well-maintained bathhouses and other facilities. A nationwide directory of KOA campgrounds, published annually, is available free at any KOA, or by mail for $3 from **Kampgrounds of America, Inc.,** Executive Offices, Billings, MT 59114-0558 (☎ **406/248-7444;** www. koa.com). Members of the **American Automobile Association (AAA)** can request the club's free *Southwestern Camp-Book,* which includes campgrounds and RV parks in Colorado, as well as Utah, Arizona, and New Mexico. Several massive campground directories can be purchased in major bookstores, including *Trailer Life Campgrounds, R.V. Parks & Services Directory,* published annually by TL Enterprises, Inc. (☎ **800/234-3450;** www.tldirectory.com), which sells for about $20.

## 6  Learning Vacations & Organized Tours

There are a number of local and national tour companies that offer tours and other activities that include Rocky Mountain National Park. In most cases, all you do is pay the company and it will arrange everything from lodging to transportation. These tours range from standard bus tours to adventure vacations where you spend your days hiking and biking. Contact tour operators far in advance of your trip since reservations are required and group sizes are limited. Trips are offered in a range of price categories and for varying lengths.

The **Rocky Mountain Nature Association** offers a wide variety of seminars and workshops, ranging from half-day to several-day programs, and **Colorado Mountain School** offers programs in technical rock and ice climbing, mountaineering, and ski mountaineering. See "Educational Programs" and "Climbing & Mountaineering," in chapter 4 for information on both organizations.

**Gorp Travel,** 1055 Westmore Drive, Suite 215, Westminster, CO 80021 (☎ **877/440-4677** or 720/887-8500; fax 303/635-0658; www.gorptravel.com), offers several 6-day guided hiking trips into and in the vicinity of Rocky Mountain National Park each summer, with lodging in local bed-and-breakfasts and inns. Participants take a somewhat leisurely excursion of 6 to 10 miles a day, giving them ample opportunity to appreciate the scenery.

**Estes Park Shuttle** (see "Getting There," above) provides 2- to 3-hour tours into Rocky Mountain National Park during the summer. Similar services are offered by **Emerald Taxi, Shuttle, Tour, and Travel Service** (☎ **970/586-1992** for taxi service, 970/586-1991 for tour information).

**Discover Colorado Scenic Tours,** 11930 W. 62nd Place, Arvada, CO 80004 (☎ **800/641-0129** or 303/425-3586; www.coloradoscenictours.com), offers personalized individual and group tours of Rocky Mountain National Park and the surrounding scenic areas and historic sites. The company offers full-day and multiday excursions and specializes in tours following lesser-used roads while stopping for picnics along the way. All of its guides are published authors.

**Gray Line,** 5855 E. 56th Ave. (P.O. Box 17527), Denver, CO 80217-0527 (☎ **800/348-6877** or 303/289-2841; fax

303/286-7052; www.coloradograyline.com), offers a 10-hour Rocky Mountain National Park guided bus tour from Denver.

**Maupintour,** 1515 St. Andrews Drive, Lawrence, KS 66047 (☎ **800/255-4266;** www.maupintour.com), offers well-planned multiday bus tours that include Rocky Mountain National Park and other scenic and historic areas.

## A RESERVATIONS SERVICE

A good compromise between doing your own thing and joining an organized tour is to work with the **Colorado Reservation Service** (☎ **800/777-6880**). Tell the destination counselors where you want to go, how long you want to stay, and how much you are willing to spend, and they will make lodging reservations for your entire trip. They can also take care of airline reservations and ground transportation, and will help arrange outdoor-activity packages.

## 7  Tips for Travelers with Disabilities

America's national parks, including Rocky Mountain, have made great strides in recent years in making their facilities more accessible to those with disabilities. At Rocky Mountain National Park, visitor centers and museums are wheelchair accessible, including the rest rooms. There are designated parking spots for travelers with disabilities, and curb cuts where necessary. A 22-minute orientation film on the park, which is shown on the lower level of the Beaver Meadows Visitor Center, is closed-captioned, although currently that section of the building is only marginally accessible because of a steep ramp.

Among the park's campgrounds, only Longs Peak and Aspenglen have no fully accessible campsites and rest rooms. There is one large accessible backcountry campsite off the Sprague Lake Trail, with a fully accessible vault toilet, picnic tables, fire ring, and grill. There are no shower facilities for anyone within the park.

Amphitheaters at Moraine Park and Aspenglen Campgrounds are fully accessible, the Glacier Basin Campground amphitheater is moderately accessible, and the amphitheater at Timber Creek has a very steep ramp that makes it only marginally accessible. Arrangements can be made in advance for preferred seating at ranger talks and similar activities.

Among the accessible trails are most of the 0.5-mile Bear Lake Trail (one section has stairs) that loops around Bear Lake, the 0.1-mile Beaver Boardwalk loop, the 0.5-mile loop around Sprague Lake, the 0.75-mile Lily Lake Loop Trail, and the 1-mile Coyote Valley Loop Trail.

A TDD phone is available at park headquarters at the Beaver Meadows Entrance, and there is also one in the **Estes Park Public Library,** 335 E. Elkhorn Ave.

The National Park Service's **Golden Access Passport,** available free at all national parks, is a lifetime pass that is issued to any U.S. citizen or permanent resident who is medically certified as disabled or blind. The pass permits free park entry and gives a 50% discount on National Park Service campgrounds and activities (not on those offered by private concessionaires).

## 8   Tips for Travelers with Pets

Rocky Mountain National Park, as well as most other federal lands administered by the National Park Service, are not pet-friendly, and those planning to visit the park should seriously consider leaving their pets at home. Dogs are prohibited on all hiking trails, in the backcountry, and in all buildings. They must always be on a leash no more than 6 feet long, and may not be taken more than 100 feet from any roadway. Pets should not be left unattended in campgrounds or alone in vehicles (owners can be fined), and owners are required to clean up after their pets. Essentially, this means that if you take your pet into the park, it can be with you in the campgrounds and inside your vehicle, and you can walk it in parking areas—but that's about it. It's no fun for either you or your pet.

Aside from regulations, though, you need to be concerned with your pet's well-being. Pets should never be left in closed vehicles, where temperatures can soar to over 100°F in minutes, resulting in brain damage or death; and no animal should ever be subjected to that kind of torture.

Those who do decide to take pets with them into the park despite the above warnings should take the pets' leashes, of course; carry plenty of water—pet shops sell clever little travel water bowls that won't spill in a moving vehicle; and proof that the dogs or cats have been vaccinated against rabies. Flea and tick spray or powder is also important.

There are no kennels inside the park. Just outside the park's
east entrance, in the community of Estes Park, there are kennel facilities at **Boarding House for Pets,** 863 Dry Gulch
Jacob Rd. (☎ **970/586-6606;** fax 970/586-2732). The **Animal Medical Center of Estes Park,** 1260 Manford Ave.
(☎ **970/586-6898**), also offers pet boarding, as well as 24-
hour emergency pet care. On the park's west side, the nearest
boarding kennel is in Granby, about 15 miles south of the
park entrance, at **Granby Veterinary Clinic,** 458 E. Agate
Ave. (☎ **970/887-3848**), which also offers complete veterinary facilities.

Although pets are not welcome on the trails or in the backcountry of Rocky Mountain National Park, leashed pets are
permitted on the trails in the Arapaho and Roosevelt national
forests, just outside the national park (see chapter 6).

## 9  Tips for Travelers with Children

Visiting Rocky Mountain National Park with your children
can be an especially rewarding experience, and it is an excellent way for everyone—children and adults alike—to learn
about the park's geology, plants, and wildlife, as well as to
appreciate the unequaled beauty of nature.

Park rangers present a number of special programs for children, aimed at helping them learn about the park's wildlife
and other natural features. Kids can obtain a Junior Ranger
guide, a logbook, and other materials from visitor centers, and
then complete various activities to become junior rangers (see
"Ranger Programs & Guided Hikes," in chapter 3).

Parents should keep in mind that there are no grocery stores
inside the park, so it's a good idea to carry a good supply of
items such as baby food and disposable diapers. Most of these
items can be purchased in Estes Park; facilities in Grand Lake
are more limited. It's also important to carry any prescription
drugs you might need, and to make sure you have the phone
numbers of your doctor and pharmacist.

## 10  Protecting Your Health & Safety

The rugged landscape that makes Rocky Mountain National
Park such a beautiful destination can also be hazardous to your
health, especially if you're not used to the extremes of climate

and altitude. Since many of the areas you'll seek out are isolated, there may be no one there to help in an emergency. The
answer is to be prepared, like any good Boy Scout (see the box
"What Should I Take?," above). Most importantly, check with
park visitor centers, rangers, and other local outdoor special-
ists about current conditions before heading out.

The main concerns for visitors are the weather and elevation. Those who have not spent time in the West's mountains
may have trouble understanding how quickly weather can
change—from a warm sunny afternoon to blizzardlike conditions in a matter of minutes—and how elevation can affect
their stamina. If you're prone to dry skin, moisturizing lotion
is a must; even if you're not, you will probably end up using
it. Everyone needs to use a good-quality sunblock, wear a hat,
and wear sunglasses with full ultraviolet protection. Hikers
and others planning to be outside will also need to carry
water—at least a gallon per person per day is recommended.

Many park visitors find that they have much less stamina
than normal, especially during their first few days in the park.
The reason for this is that there's less oxygen and lower
humidity up in the mountains than most of us are accustomed
to. Those with heart or respiratory problems should consult
their doctors before planning a trip to the mountains. If you're
generally healthy, you don't need to take any special precautions, although it's advisable to ease into the high elevations by
changing altitude gradually, perhaps by spending a few days in
Denver, at 5,280 feet, before venturing into the park. Also, get
plenty of rest, avoid large meals, and drink plenty of nonalcoholic fluids, especially water. There are prescription drugs
that can help ease the transition to higher elevations; consult
your doctor several weeks before leaving home.

Afternoon thunderstorms are fairly common in the park,
especially during July and August, when visitors should avoid
mountaintops, ridges, and other open areas to minimize the
risk of being struck by lightning. Lightning is not the only
concern: visibility becomes difficult in rain or snow, and hikers have been known to accidentally step off terra firma into
nothingness, with fatal results.

Hikers, especially those venturing into lesser-used areas of
the backcountry, need to be careful to avoid confrontations
with **mountain lions.** When entering lion country (rangers

---

### Warning: You Are in Bear Country!

If a bear enters or approaches your campsite, or approaches you while you're on a trail:

- Stay calm.
- Don't run, but move slowly away from the bear.
- Look carefully to make sure you are not getting between a mother and her cub.
- Make noise by clanging pots and pans together, clapping your hands, or shouting.
- If possible, put any exposed food in airtight containers.
- Report the bear sighting to a park ranger.

---

can advise you on specific areas where mountain lions have recently been seen), travel in groups and make plenty of noise. Keep children with you at all times; and if you do see a mountain lion, stop but do not run. Raise your arms to try to appear as large as possible and then back away slowly.

In recent years problems with **black bears** have been increasing, in part because below-average precipitation has caused a shortage of the berries and other foods the bears usually eat, but also because the bears have learned that where there are humans there is food. Although generally less aggressive than mountain lions, bears can be dangerous, and you'll want to be wary of them. First and foremost, do not get between a mother bear and her cub. Also, do not leave food or anything that might smell like food in a tent—store food in airtight containers in a car trunk. It's both foolhardy and illegal to feed bears or any other wildlife, or to leave food unattended. Rangers warn that pepper spray does not deter bears; in fact, some types of pepper spray actually attract bears. Bears are also attracted by perfumes and other scented products, and some bear experts add that even the smell of humans having sexual relations can attract bears.

Another potentially hazardous form of wildlife in Rocky Mountain National Park is *Giardia,* a microscopic organism that is found in lakes, streams, and possibly even snow. In humans, it can cause diarrhea, cramps, bloating, and weight loss. To avoid problems, backcountry campers and hikers should not drink lake or stream water, or even melted snow, without bringing it to a full rolling boil for a minimum of 3 to 5 minutes or without using another reliable water-purification system.

Hikers will also want to avoid **ticks.** These are found mostly in brushy and wooded areas; they attach themselves to the skin and drink their victims' blood. Use a tick repellent on your lower legs, and wear light-colored clothing so you can more easily spot ticks. Inspect your skin well during and after outings. Remove a tick with tweezers, after putting oil or ointment on it to cut off its air supply, and be careful to remove the entire tick in one piece. Only a small percentage of ticks carry disease, although several hundred cases of Colorado tick fever are reported each year. If you are unable to completely remove a tick from your skin, or if a rash develops or you become achy or nauseous, consult a physician.

Health officials warn outdoor enthusiasts to take precautions against **bubonic plague,** which was known as the Black Death during the Middle Ages. The plague is frequently detected in wood rats, rock squirrels, prairie dogs, chipmunks, and other rodents throughout the western United States, including Rocky Mountain National Park. Avoiding contact with infected animals will greatly minimize the chances of contracting the plague, but caution is still necessary. Those taking pets into the park should dust them with flea and tick powder. Contrary to popular belief, bubonic plague is treatable with antibiotics if caught early. Symptoms, which generally occur 2 to 6 days after exposure, may include high fever, headache, vomiting, diarrhea, and swollen glands. Anyone with these symptoms following a park visit should get immediate medical attention, because the plague can be fatal if not treated promptly.

Another potential health concern is the **hantavirus,** a rare but often-fatal respiratory disease, first recognized in 1993. About half of the country's several hundred confirmed cases have been reported in the Four Corners states of Colorado, New Mexico, Arizona, and Utah. The disease is usually spread by the urine and droppings of rodents, and health officials recommend that campers avoid areas with signs of rodent occupation. Symptoms of hantavirus are similar to flu, and lead to breathing difficulties and shock.

## 11  Protecting the Environment

Many of the wonderful outdoor areas you'll be exploring in Rocky Mountain National Park are quite isolated. Although you're certainly not the first human being to set foot there, you may feel as though you are. Not too long ago, the rule of thumb was "leave only footprints"; these days, we're trying to do better and not leave even footprints. It's relatively easy to be a good outdoor citizen—mostly common sense. Pack out all trash, stay on established trails, be especially careful to not pollute water, and, in general, do your best to have as little impact on the environment as possible. Some hikers go further, carrying a small trash bag to pick up what others may have left.

Because of the vast quantity of wildlife in the park, human visitors need to be especially careful to protect these park residents. Do not feed any animals—even those cute little chipmunks and ground squirrels that have become so skilled at begging. At the very least it robs them of their own survival skills; at worst, it may seriously harm them or lead to human injuries or disease. View and photograph animals from roadways, and never approach them; and do not shine automobile headlights or portable spotlights on wildlife. In short, as visitors—actually intruders—into these animals' home, make every effort to disturb them as little as possible, and let wild things remain truly wild.

# 3

# Exploring Rocky Mountain National Park

*T*he best of the Rocky Mountains is captured in this high mountain national park, located along the Continental Divide in north-central Colorado. Established in 1915, the park can be seen in various ways, from the safety of a car driving along Trail Ridge Road, or from a precarious perch on the edge of an icy wall of rock. To get an overall view of the park, most visitors combine a car trip with at least several walks and hikes, and we suggest that you do this as well.

Although Trail Ridge Road is Rocky's main attraction, and certainly the easiest way to see the park's famous alpine tundra, don't neglect other sections of the park, such as Bear Lake Road, which provides excellent views and leads to several particularly scenic hiking trails. Perhaps the best piece of advice we can give, though, is to refrain from rushing through the entire park in a single visit. Take your time and get to know a bit of the park more intimately, and on its own terms.

## 1 Essentials

**ACCESS/ENTRY POINTS**   Entry into the park is from either the east (through the town of Estes Park) or the west (through the town of Grand Lake). The east and west sides of the park are connected by Trail Ridge Road, open during summer and early fall, but closed to all motor-vehicle traffic by snow the rest of the year. Most visitors enter the park from the Estes Park side. The Beaver Meadows Entrance, west of Estes Park via U.S. 36, leads to the Beaver Meadows Visitor Center and park headquarters, and is the most direct route to Trail Ridge Road. U.S. 34 west from Estes Park takes you to the Fall River Visitor Center, just outside the park, and into the park via the Fall River Entrance, which is north of the Beaver Meadows Entrance. From there you can access Old Fall River Road or Trail Ridge Road.

# Rocky Mountain National Park

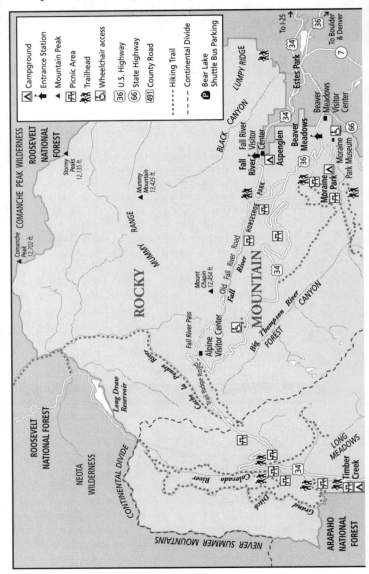

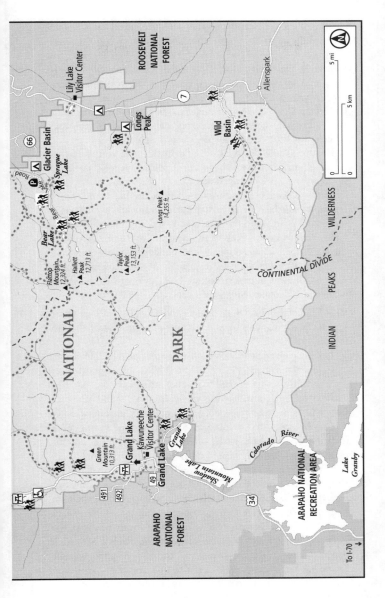

ROOSEVELT NATIONAL FOREST

Lily Lake
Visitor Center

Longs Peak

Wild Basin

Allenspark

7

66

Glacier Basin

Sprague
Lake

Bear
Lake

Bear Lake Road

P

Flattop
Mountain,
12,324 ft.

Hallett
Peak
12,713 ft.

Taylor
Peak
13,153 ft.

Longs Peak
14,255 ft.

NATIONAL

CONTINENTAL DIVIDE

PARK

INDIAN          PEAKS          WILDERNESS

Green
Mountain
10,313 ft.

Kawuneeche
Visitor Center

Grand
Lake

Grand Lake

Shadow Mountain Lake

Colorado River

491

492

49

34

ARAPAHO
NATIONAL
FOREST

ARAPAHO NATIONAL
RECREATION AREA

Lake
Granby

To I-70

N

0                    5 mi

0                    5 km

Old Fall River Road, which is a 9-mile gravel road, is one-way uphill (west) only, and is usually open from July 4 to mid-October. It connects to Trail Ridge Road at the Alpine Visitor Center at Fall River Pass. Bear Lake Road, just west of the Beaver Meadows Entrance, is the access road to Bear Lake and is open year-round, but it can be icy and snowpacked in winter. In summer, a free national park **shuttle bus** runs along Bear Lake Road, with departures every 15 to 30 minutes. Check at visitor centers for the current schedule.

Heading south from Estes Park on Colo. 7, you can access two trailheads in the southeast corner of the national park, but there are no connecting roads to the main part of the park from those points. These are Longs Peak trailhead (the turnoff is 9 miles south of Estes Park and the trailhead about another mile) and Wild Basin trailhead (another 3.5 miles south along Colo. 7 from Longs Peak to the turnoff and then 2.5 miles to the trailhead). Those entering the park from the west should take U.S. 40 north from I-70 through Winter Park and Tabernash to Granby, and then follow U.S. 34 north to the village of Grand Lake and the park entrance.

**VISITOR CENTERS & INFORMATION**    When entering the park, it's wise to make your first stop one of the visitor centers.

The **Beaver Meadows Visitor Center,** on U.S. 36 on the east side of the park (☎ **970/586-1206**), has a good interpretive exhibit that includes a relief model of the park, an audiovisual program, a wide choice of books and maps for sale, and knowledgeable people to answer questions and give advice. A self-guided nature trail just outside the visitor center identifies many of the park's plants. In summer it's open daily from 8am to 9pm; in winter, daily from 8am to 5pm.

Just outside the park, on U.S. 34 and just east of the Fall River entrance on the east side of the national park, is the new **Fall River Visitor Center,** which was completed in the summer of 2000. Located in a beautiful mountain lodge-style building, it was constructed with private funds but is staffed by park rangers and volunteers from the Rocky Mountain Nature Association. It contains exhibits on park wildlife, including some spectacular full-size bronzes of elk and other animals, plus an activity/discovery room for children, an information desk, and a bookstore. It's open in summer only, daily from 8am to 8pm. Next door is **Rocky Mountain**

## Numbers, Numbers, Numbers

**Size of the park:** 265,723 acres or 415.2 square miles

**Designated wilderness:** 2,917 acres

**Highest recorded visitation:** 3,366,253, in 1999

**Law enforcement** (traffic accidents, arrests, citations, warnings): 1,588 in 1999, 1,534 in 1998, 1,415 in 1997, 2,020 in 1996

**Major rescues:** 25 in 1999, 21 in 1998, 16 in 1997, 15 in 1996

**Fatalities:** seven in 1999, three in 1998, six in 1997, two in 1996

**Emergency medical services:** 256 in 1999, 216 in 1998

**Number of lakes:** 147

**Number of lakes containing fish:** 50

**Annual precipitation:** 14.79 inches on the east side, 20.36 inches on the west side

**Roads:** 63 miles paved, 20 miles unpaved

**Trails:** 347 miles

**Buildings:** two museums, five visitor centers, five amphitheaters, 31 rest rooms, 144 employee residences

**Picnic tables:** 176

**Park employees:** 140 permanent, 275 temporary (1999)

**Volunteers:** 1,687 people donating 81,108 hours (1999)

**Gateway** (☎ 970/577-0043), a large and somewhat pricey souvenir-and-clothing shop that also contains a cafeteria-style restaurant with snacks and sandwiches.

The **Kawuneeche Visitor Center** (open in summer, daily from 8am to 6pm; winter, daily from 8am to 4:30pm) is located at the Grand Lake end of Trail Ridge Road (☎ 970/627-3471). In addition to exhibits on the geology, plants, animals, and human history of the park's west side, there is a small theater where films and video programs are shown, and a short self-guided nature trail. By the way, *kawuneeche* (kah-wuh-*nee*-chee) is an Arapaho word that translates as "valley of the coyote."

The **Alpine Visitor Center** (open in summer only, daily from 9am to 5pm) at Fall River Pass, has exhibits that explain life on the alpine tundra and a viewing platform from which you are almost certain to see elk. Next door is the Fall River Store, open in summer, with a snack bar and large gift shop that has an especially good selection of souvenirs, gifts, arts and crafts, and clothing, at surprisingly reasonable prices. The **Moraine Park Museum** (open mid-April to mid-October, daily from 9am to 5pm) is located on Bear Lake Road in a historic log building that dates from 1923. It has full visitor-center facilities, in addition to excellent natural-history exhibits that describe the creation of the park's landscape, as well as the plants and animals of the park. There's also a nature trail outside. The **Lily Lake Visitor Center** (open June through September, daily from 9am to 4pm) is located along Colo. 7 about 7 miles south of Estes Park. In addition to information on the national park, it has exhibits and information on activities in the adjacent Roosevelt and Arapaho national forests.

**ENTRANCE/CAMPING FEES**   Park admission costs $15 per vehicle for up to 1 week; $5 for bicyclists, motorcyclists, and pedestrians. An annual park pass costs $30. Campers will pay $16 per night during the summer in the park's developed campgrounds and $10 in the off-season (when the water is turned off, usually from late September to mid-May). Permits are required at all times for overnight trips into the backcountry and include camping at the park's designated backcountry and bivouac campsites. The cost is $15 from May through October; the permits are free the rest of the year. (See "Exploring the Backcountry," in chapter 4, for details.)

**SPECIAL REGULATIONS/WARNINGS**   Rocky Mountain National Park's high elevation and varying climate and terrain are among its most appealing features, but also are responsible for some of its greatest hazards. Hikers should try to give themselves a minimum of several days to acclimate to the altitude before seriously hitting the trails, and those with respiratory or heart problems should discuss their plans with their physicians before leaving home. Hikers also need to be prepared for rapidly changing conditions, particularly the sudden afternoon thunderstorms in July and August. If lightning threatens, everyone is well advised to stay clear of ridges and other vulnerable high points. (See the sections "Climate & Weather" and "Protecting Your Health & Safety," in chapter 2.)

## Where to Find Rest Rooms

The all-important rest rooms at Rocky Mountain National Park are generally well maintained but vary considerably in the facilities offered. As at most national parks, the best are at the visitor centers and museums, where you'll find heated rooms with flush toilets and sinks with hot water.

Along Trail Ridge Road there are vault toilets at Rainbow Curve Overlook, the trailhead for Tundra Nature Trail, Rock Cut, Fall River Pass, Milner Pass, Colorado River Trailhead, Timber Lake Trailhead, Never Summer Ranch, Bowen/Baker Gulch Trailhead, Green Mountain Trailhead, Coyote Valley Trailhead, and East Inlet Trailhead. There are flush toilets with cold-water sinks at all of the park's developed campgrounds and the Bear Lake Trailhead, which are open in summer only. Once freezing temperatures arrive, only vault toilets are available. There are also vault toilets in other areas throughout the park.

Although essentially outhouses, vault toilets have come a long way in the past 20 years—now they're clean, they're sanitary, and, best of all, they don't smell. However, they have no lights and no heat, and although vault toilets do not have water for hand washing, most of those in the park do provide waterless hand soap.

During busy times, the less-developed rest room facilities may run out of toilet paper, so it's best to carry a small packet of facial tissues or a similar backup source of this important commodity.

Special rules instituted by the National Park Service at Rocky Mountain National Park include the following:

- It is illegal to disturb or damage any natural features, cultural resources, or other public property. This includes potsherds, arrowheads, rocks, old wood, and pieces of mining equipment.
- Feeding, touching, or harassing wildlife is prohibited; no hunting is allowed within park boundaries. It is illegal to use motor vehicle headlights or other lights to spot wildlife.
- Weapons and fireworks are prohibited.
- Berry picking for immediate consumption is permitted, but all other picking, collecting, or damaging of plants (including the picking of wildflowers) is prohibited.

- Camping is permitted only in designated areas.
- Vehicles must remain on roads or in designated parking areas, and stopping or parking is permitted only in designated areas. Colorado driving laws, including seat-belt and child-restraint laws, are enforced. It is illegal to have open containers of alcoholic beverages in a vehicle while on park roads.
- Bikes are permitted on park roads and in parking areas, but not on trails or in the backcountry.
- Leaving property (vehicles, tents, and so on) unattended for longer than 24 hours without prior permission is prohibited.
- Pets must be under physical control at all times and cannot be left unattended, even in vehicles; pets are not permitted on trails, in the backcountry, or in buildings. Owners must clean up after their pets.
- All anglers 15 and older must possess valid Colorado fishing licenses. Adults must use artificial lures or flies in park waters; children 12 and under can use bait in open park waters, but not in catch-and-release areas.

## FAST FACTS: Rocky Mountain National Park

**ATMs**    Although there are no automatic teller machines within the park boundaries, they are easy to find in banks and grocery stores in the gateway towns of Estes Park and Grand Lake. For instance, there is one at the **Safeway** grocery store, 451 E. Wonderview Ave., in Stanley Village Center (☎ **970/ 586-4447**) in Estes Park, just minutes from the park entrance.

**Car Trouble/Towing Services**    There are no towing or repair facilities inside the park. For towing and repairs on the east side of the park, contact **Bob's Amoco,** 172 W. Elkhorn Ave., Estes Park (☎ **970/586-3122**), which offers 24-hour towing and road service, and has equipment capable of towing motor homes, RVs, and other large vehicles.

On the west side of the park, 24-hour towing and emergency road repairs are offered by **DJ Towing** in Granby (☎ **970/887-9414**), which can handle most motor homes and other large vehicles.

**Emergencies**    Dial ☎ 911 or park headquarters at ☎ **970/ 586-1399.** There are **Emergency Call Boxes** at Bear Lake Parking Lot, Cow Creek Trailhead, Hidden Valley Ranger Station, Lawn Lake Trailhead, Longs Peak Ranger Station, and

Wild Basin Ranger Station. The statewide **Poison Control Hotline** is ☎ **800/332-3073.**

**Gas Stations**    There are no gas stations in the park, but just outside both east entrances in Estes Park, you'll find most major gasoline brands represented. In Grand Lake, just outside the park's west entrance, there are several gas stations; and you'll find a wider selection in Granby, about 14 miles to the south.

**Laundries**    There are no laundry facilities inside the park. On the east side of the park, just outside the Fall River Entrance Station, there is a coin-operated laundry adjacent to the Fall River Visitor Center at **Rocky Mountain Gateway** (see "Supplies," below). You'll also find coin-operated washers and dryers, including machines that can accommodate sleeping bags and other large items, at **Dad's Maytag Laundry,** in Upper Stanley Village Center in Estes Park (☎ **970/586-2025**), which also offers drop-off service, public showers, and a customer lounge with a television. From Memorial Day to mid-August it's open daily from 7am to 9:30pm; the rest of the year it's open daily from 7:30am to 7:30pm.

In Grand Lake, on the west side of the national park, the self-serve, coin-operated **Mountain Village Laundromat,** 701 Grand Ave. (☎ **970/887-3719**), is located next to Circle D grocery store. In addition to standard-size washers and dryers, there are several large units for sleeping bags and similar items. Hours in summer are 8am to 10pm daily, and winter hours are daily from 8am to 9pm.

**Medical Services**    On the east side of the national park, **Estes Park Medical Center,** with a 24-hour emergency room, is at 555 Prospect Ave. (☎ **970/586-2317**). Those with medical problems on the west side of the park will need to travel 14 miles from the park entrance to **Centura Health Granby Medical Center,** 480 E. Agate Ave., Granby (☎ **970/887-2117**), which offers 24-hour emergency care.

**Photographic Supplies**    There are no camera-repair facilities in either of the park's gateway towns. You'll find film in many grocery and convenience stores. But for a better choice of film, and for photo processing, camera batteries, filters and other accessories, and cameras (including disposable), stop at **Western One Hour Photo,** 101 W. Elkhorn Ave., Estes Park (☎ **970/586-8522**).

**Post Offices**   There are mail drops at the Beaver Meadows and Kawuneeche visitor centers. A full-service U.S. Post Office is located in Estes Park (ZIP 80517) at 215 W. Riverside Dr., and in Grand Lake (ZIP 80447) at 520 Center Dr. For the hours and the locations of other area post offices, contact the U.S. Postal Service (☎ **800/275-8777**).

**Supplies**   The **Country Supermarket,** 900 Moraine Ave., Estes Park (☎ **970/586-2702**), is located just 0.75 mile from the Beaver Meadows entrance to the park in a small shopping center. The store has a good stock of groceries, including fresh meats and produce, a deli and an ATM machine, ice and firewood, and a large RV-accessible parking lot. It is open daily from 7am to 10pm in summer, from 7am to 9pm the rest of the year. Outside the Fall River Entrance Station, adjacent to the new Fall River Visitor Center, **Rocky Mountain Gateway,** 3450 Fall River Rd. (☎ **970/577-0043**), contains a large gift shop, restaurant, convenience store with groceries, camping supplies, clothing, ice, firewood, and a self-serve laundry. Daily midsummer hours are 8am to 8pm, and hours are somewhat shorter the rest of the year.

Those looking for top-quality camping and outdoor sports equipment should stop at **Outdoor World,** downtown at 156 E. Elkhorn Ave. (☎ **970/586-2114**), which sells all sorts of backpacking equipment and outdoor gear, including hiking boots, outdoor clothing, maps, and supplies. It also rents equipment, such as backpacks, day-packs, hikers' baby carriers, sleeping bags, tents, and snowshoes. Across the street from Outdoor World, under the same management, is the larger **Rocky Mountain Connection,** 141 E. Elkhorn Ave. (☎ **800/ 679-3600** or 970/586-3361; www.rmconnection.com), which carries many of the same items as Outdoor World plus a large inventory of casual and outdoor clothing. Both stores are open daily from 9am to 10pm in summer and close slightly earlier the rest of the year.

Another good choice for outdoor gear is **Estes Park Mountain Shop,** 358 E. Elkhorn Ave. (☎ **800/504-6642** or 970/ 586-6548), which has a store with sales and rental departments and an indoor climbing gym. The retail sales department sells hiking and camping equipment, winter sports items, fishing supplies and licenses, and outdoor clothing. You can also rent camping gear such as tents, sleeping bags, snow-shoes, cross-country skis, and downhill skis. The company offers fly-fishing and climbing instruction and guided trips both in and around the national park. It also offers a kids' outdoor adventure program in half- and full-day sessions (see chapter 4). Daily hours are from 9am to 9pm year-round.

In Grand Lake, on the park's west side, the **Mountain Food Market,** 400 Grand Ave. (☎ **970/627-3470**), and the **Circle D,** 701 Grand Ave. (☎ **970/627-3210**), have good selections of groceries and picnic supplies. You can get picnic and fishing supplies, and almost anything else you might need, at **Grand Lake Pharmacy,** 1123 Grand Ave. (☎ **970/627-3465**). Hours at these Grand Lake establishments vary; call for the current schedule.

**Telephones**   There are public telephones at park visitor centers and museums, and at all campgrounds except Longs Peak. The park also has emergency call boxes (see "Emergencies," above).

**Weather & Road-Condition Updates**   Within the park call ☎ **970/586-1333** or tune your radio to 1610 AM. In Estes Park, you can call ☎ **970/586-5555** for information, which includes weather and road conditions for the town as well as the park; for statewide road conditions, call ☎ **303/639-1111** in Denver. Statewide road conditions are also available on the Web at **www.cotrip.com**.

## 2   Tips from a Park Ranger

The ease with which visitors can experience the many faces of Rocky Mountain National Park helps make it a very special place, according to park spokesman Dick Putney.

There are other alpine tundra areas in the United States, but you usually have to do a lot of hard hiking, Putney says. "What makes Rocky Mountain National Park unique is that Trail Ridge Road takes you up to the tundra—above tree line—in the comfort of your car; you can see plant and animal communities that if not for this park you would have to go to the Arctic Circle to see."

Those willing and able to hike can see plenty of tundra country. Putney suggests having a friend drop you off at the

**Ute Trail** turnout on Trail Ridge Road, where you can hike the 6 miles down through Forest Canyon to Upper Beaver Meadows. He says this canyon is among the wildest in the park, adding that the hike along its steep side provides spectacular views of the canyon and Longs Peak, the park's tallest mountain.

Another hike that Putney recommends is the 2-mile (one-way) **Gem Lake Trail,** on the park's east side. "When you're going up that trail, there are several places to look across the Estes Valley to Longs Peak, and the lake is a wonderful spot for a picnic," he says. Those who want to work a bit harder will be well rewarded on another of Putney's favorites, the East Inlet Trail on the west side of the park. "Once you get up there a couple of miles, and gain some elevation, you look back toward Grand Lake and think you're in Switzerland."

**Longs Peak,** at 14,255 feet elevation, is the northernmost of Colorado's famed "fourteeners" (mountains that exceed 14,000 ft. elevation), and it's a popular hike, maintains Putney. "You don't need technical climbing gear once the ice is gone—usually by mid-July," Putney says, adding that hikers may have some physical problems with the altitude at first. "It's wise to give yourself at least a couple of days to acclimate before tackling Longs Peak," Putney says. He also recommends that high-elevation hikers drink plenty of nonalcoholic fluids, eat regularly, carry energy bars, take it slow, and listen to their bodies. Another tip he gives backpackers is to spend time discussing their plans with rangers in the park's Backcountry Office before setting out. "We'd much rather spend time with them beforehand to try to get to know their abilities and expectations, and advise them where to go, than be called out on a search-and-rescue mission."

"One activity that many visitors miss out on is viewing the night sky," says Putney. He suggests taking a picnic supper and stopping at one of the Trail Ridge Road **viewpoints** after dark, when most park visitors are in their motel rooms or campsites. "We don't have any light pollution here," he says. "You think you can just reach up and touch the Milky Way. You can see satellites, and the Perseids meteor shower in August is something you won't soon forget."

Putney says the easiest method to avoid crowds, even during the park's busiest season, is to take off down a hiking trail, since most visitors remain close to the roads. "The farther you go up the trail, the fewer people you'll encounter," he says. He adds that another sure way to escape humanity is to visit in winter, and explore the park on snowshoes or cross-country skis.

And when would he visit? "Fall—from September through mid-October—is the best time," he says. "Days are warm and comfortable, nights are cool and crisp, there are fewer people than in summer, and the aspens are changing. You can see hundreds of elk, and watch the bulls bugle as they protect their harems from the other bulls. But, it might snow!"

## 3  The Highlights

Because Rocky is such a vast and varied national park, it's difficult to say what the highlights are; it's hard to identify the things that every park visitor must see and do. However, it is worth noting several of the park's major attractions. One must take a trip over **Trail Ridge Road,** a spectacularly scenic drive through the park that goes across the Continental Divide and above the tree line into a land of alpine tundra that most of us have never seen. Another must-see is **Longs Peak,** the park's highest mountain, which can be seen from a variety of locations. There is an especially good (and easily accessible) view of the peak from the Moraine Park Museum.

For many people, the highlight of a park visit is a trip to one of its numerous **mountain lakes,** whose beautiful reflections of the surrounding forests and mountains are often enhanced by snowcapped peaks. Practically any of the park's lakes will do, although we particularly enjoy the views across the easy-to-get-to Sprague and Bear lakes.

It's our hope that every visitor to the park gets to see some **wildlife,** particularly the larger animals such as elk, deer, moose (on the west side), and the park's symbol—Rocky Mountain bighorn sheep. What you'll see depends in part on the time of year you visit and whether you'll be hiking or staying close to the roadways, so check with rangers on the best spots and time of day for your particular circumstances.

## 4  How to See the Park in Several Days

### IF YOU HAVE ONLY 1 OR 2 DAYS

Although this is a park that simply begs for an extended visit—
4 to 7 days would allow you the time to stop at viewpoints, see
the exhibits, and hike at least a few trails—it also has the
advantage of offering a wonderful experience to visitors who
have only a short time, or who are not able or willing to hike.

Those arriving in summer or early fall with only a day to see
the park will want to stop at one of the visitor centers, and
then drive the fantastically scenic **Trail Ridge Road,** described
below. Stop at the viewpoints and take the half-hour walk
along the **Tundra World Nature Trail** to get a close-up view
of the plants, animals, and terrain of this rocky yet fragile
world. Those returning to the east or west sides will have time
for little else, since it takes about 3 hours each way for the 48-
mile drive, but those passing through the park on their way to
somewhere else may want to take another of the park's many
hikes (see "East-Side Day Hikes" and "West-Side Day Hikes,"
in chapter 4).

Having gotten a good overview of the grand scheme of
Rocky Mountain National Park during your first day's drive
on Trail Ridge Road, on your second day it's time for a close-
up. If you're camping in the park or staying nearby, you may
want to spend your first evening at one of the **amphitheater
programs** presented by park rangers. For your second day,
check out the schedule for **guided hikes** and other ranger-led
activities, or make the drive to **Bear Lake,** taking time along
the way for a look at the natural-history exhibits at the
**Moraine Park Museum** and an easy walk around **Sprague
Lake.** From the Bear Lake Trailhead, you can take a leisurely
walk around Bear Lake, or strike out on one of the moderately
rated hiking trails, such as the trail to scenic **Emerald Lake,**
that are described in the next chapter.

### IF YOU HAVE 3 OR MORE DAYS

On your third day, you could attempt a more strenuous hike,
such as the **East Inlet Trail** to Lake Verna or Spirit Lake, on
the west side of the park. Summer visitors looking for some
less-physical adventures may prefer a drive up the steep, gravel
**Old Fall River Road,** a trip that gives you a feel for the
ruggedness of the park from the comfort of your car.

That afternoon a visit to the historic **Never Summer Ranch** for a talk by a park ranger might be in order. If you're visiting in early fall, you'll want to take time in the late afternoon and early evening to drive to the various **elk-viewing** areas to see the bulls guarding their harems, and bugling their displeasure at any other bulls who approach.

Those fortunate enough to have additional time in the park will probably hike additional trails, may possibly take some overnight backcountry treks, and may even attempt to conquer Longs Peak, the park's tallest mountain.

## 5  Driving Tours

Although Rocky Mountain National Park is often considered the domain of hikers and climbers, it's surprisingly easy to enjoy all of the park's offerings without working up a sweat. For that we thank **Trail Ridge Road.** Built in 1932 and undoubtedly one of America's most scenic highways, it provides expansive and sometimes dizzying views in all directions. This remarkable 48-mile road partially follows routes traveled by early Paleo-Indians and later Arapahos and Utes. It passes through all the park's ecosystems, crosses the Continental Divide, and climbs well above the tree line to a barren land where the plants, animals, and even weather are similar to those of the Arctic Circle. Along the way it offers spectacular views of snow-capped peaks, deep forests, and meadows of wildflowers where sheep, elk, and deer graze.

To avoid the crowds, start out on Trail Ridge Road as early in the morning as possible. As an added benefit, you'll have a much better chance of seeing wildlife if you're on the road by 7 or 8am. Allow at least 3 hours for the drive, and consider a short walk or hike from one of the many vista points. Be aware that those accustomed to lower elevations may experience some dizziness when they step from their vehicles. Also, keep a jacket or sweater within reach, regardless of how warm it may be when you set out; temperatures drop as you climb and weather changes rapidly in these mountains.

Trail Ridge Road is closed by winter snows, with drifts sometimes towering as high as 50 feet. It usually closes around mid-October before clearing in late May. But even in the summer, the road can be closed by snow for hours or even days at a time.

# Rocky Mountain National Park Activities

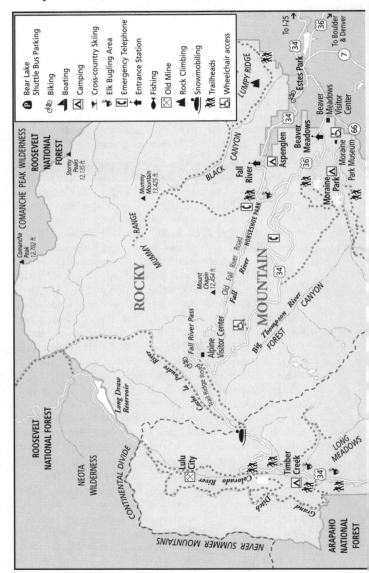

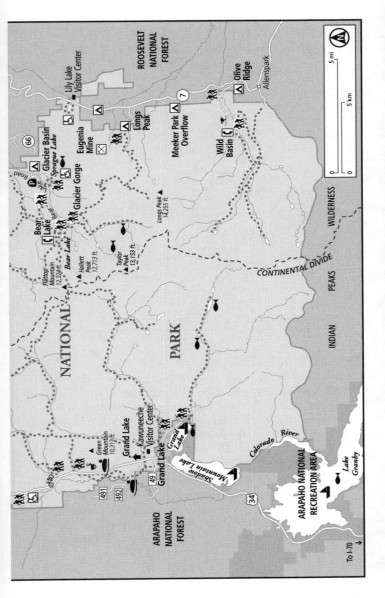

ROOSEVELT NATIONAL FOREST

Lily Lake Visitor Center

Glacier Basin

Sprague Lake

66

Eugenia Mine

Longs Peak

7

Meeker Park Overflow

Olive Ridge

Allenspark

Wild Basin

Bear Lake Road

Glacier Gorge

Bear Lake

Flattop Mountain 12,324 ft.

Hallett Peak 12,713 ft.

Longs Peak ▲ 14,255 ft.

Taylor Peak 13,153 ft.

NATIONAL

CONTINENTAL DIVIDE

PARK

INDIAN PEAKS WILDERNESS

Green Mountain 10,313 ft.

Kawuneeche Visitor Center

Grand Lake

Grand Lake

Grand Lake

491

492

49

34

ARAPAHO NATIONAL FOREST

Shadow Mountain Lake

Colorado River

ARAPAHO NATIONAL RECREATION AREA

Lake Granby

To I-70 →

N

5 mi

5 km

# Trail Ridge Road

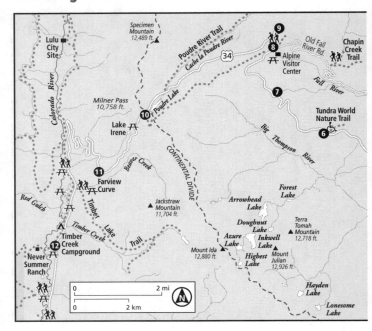

## ✪ TRAIL RIDGE ROAD

Along Trail Ridge Road are numbered signs, from 1 to 12, starting on the east side of the park and heading west. These stops are described below, and the route is also discussed in a brochure available at park visitor centers (25¢). Motorists starting from the west side of the park will begin at number 12 and count down. You'll find additional information on the historic sites in the "Historic Attractions" section, later in this chapter.

**Stop No. 1: Deer Ridge Junction.** This spot offers views of the Mummy Mountain Range to the north, and it is the official beginning of Trail Ridge Road, the highest continuous paved road in the United States, reaching an elevation of 12,183 feet. Here you're only at a mere 8,940 feet.

**Stop No. 2: Hidden Valley.** Formerly the site of a downhill ski area, this scenic subalpine valley boasts forests of Engelmann spruce and fir. The elevation is 9,240 feet.

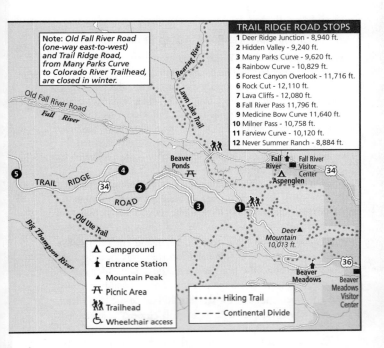

Note: Old Fall River Road (one-way east-to-west) and Trail Ridge Road, from Many Parks Curve to Colorado River Trailhead, are closed in winter.

**TRAIL RIDGE ROAD STOPS**

1 Deer Ridge Junction - 8,940 ft.
2 Hidden Valley - 9,240 ft.
3 Many Parks Curve - 9,620 ft.
4 Rainbow Curve - 10,829 ft.
5 Forest Canyon Overlook - 11,716 ft.
6 Rock Cut - 12,110 ft.
7 Lava Cliffs - 12,080 ft.
8 Fall River Pass 11,796 ft.
9 Medicine Bow Curve 11,640 ft.
10 Milner Pass - 10,758 ft.
11 Farview Curve - 10,120 ft.
12 Never Summer Ranch - 8,884 ft.

Roaring River

Old Fall River Road
Fall River

Lawn Lake Trail

Beaver Ponds

Fall River

Fall River Visitor Center
Aspenglen

5 TRAIL RIDGE 4

34

2

ROAD 3 1

Old Ute Trail

Big Thompson River

Deer Mountain 10,013 ft.

Beaver Meadows

36

Beaver Meadows Visitor Center

▲ Campground
✝ Entrance Station
▲ Mountain Peak
⛱ Picnic Area
🚶 Trailhead
♿ Wheelchair access

•••••• Hiking Trail
----- Continental Divide

**Stop No. 3: ✪ Many Parks Curve.** This delightfully scenic stop, with one of the best roadside views in the park, is also a good location for bird-watchers, who are likely to spot the noisy Steller's jay and Clark's nutcracker. The term "park" is used for its definition as a level valley between mountain ranges, often an open grassy area, which in this case was carved by glaciers some 10,000 years ago. The elevation is 9,620 feet.

**Stop No. 4: Rainbow Curve.** Just past a sign announcing your position 2 miles above sea level is Rainbow Curve, an area known for colorful rainbows that are often seen after thunderstorms. It's also famous for ferocious winds and brutal winters. Take a look at the trees that have branches only on their downwind side, where they are protected from the elements by their trunks. The excellent view from the overlook here extends past Longs Peak and into Hidden Valley and

### ✪ Old Fall River Road: A Step Back in Time

For those who find Trail Ridge Road too civilized or too easy, there is an alternative: The park's original road is still here for the driving, and it's still mostly dirt, still steep, and just as narrow and winding as ever. Covering 11 miles (two paved and nine gravel), from Horseshoe Park to Fall River Pass, this one-way (west) road climbs 3,200 feet, providing today's visitors with a glimpse into the experiences of those who explored this rugged land in Model T Fords and Stanley Steamers during its early years as a national park.

Even before the establishment of Rocky Mountain National Park in 1915, there was interest in building a road through the mountains, and in July 1913, work began with the arrival of 38 convicts from the Colorado State Penitentiary. The road was finally dedicated on September 14, 1920, and until Trail Ridge Road was built in 1932, Old Fall River Road was the only route from the east into the heart of the national park. In actuality, although the grading was new, the route of Old Fall River Road was not, since it followed what Arapahos called the Dog's Trail, a path where they used dogs to pull crude V-shaped sleds through the mountains.

Today this road remains much the way it was in the 1920s, with numerous drop-offs and switchbacks—not for anyone with a serious fear of heights! As you drive it, you'll see boulder fields, riparian areas, and cascading waterfalls, as well as some of the most rugged high-elevation sections of the park. Watch for the stone walls along the roadsides that were built during the 1920s in an often-unsuccessful effort to keep the road from being washed away. Snowmelt, freezing and thawing, and thunderstorms often caused damage to the road. A mud slide in July 1953 did so much harm that the park service was ready to give up on the road; but public pressure led the powers-that-be to have a change of heart, and the historic Old Fall River Road was reopened in 1968.

Horseshoe Park, where you can see rock, gravel, and other rubble left by a flood that struck in 1982 after a dam broke. The elevation is 10,829 feet.

Passing through three ecosystems, the relatively short (albeit slow) drive provides a cross-section view of Rocky Mountain National Park, its plants and animals, its forests and valleys, and its famous alpine tundra, quite likely the bleakest, but most fascinating, terrain most people will ever see. Open only in summer, Old Fall River Road begins at an elevation of 8,558 feet in what is called the **montane** ecosystem. One of the milder sections of the park, it is home to ponderosa pine, Douglas fir, quaking aspen, numerous birds, and a wide variety of mammals ranging from cotton-tail rabbits to elk and mountain lions. Continue your drive and you'll soon ease into the **subalpine** ecosystem, which is cooler and more moist than the montane, with forests of Engelmann spruce, Colorado blue spruce, and subalpine fir. You'll find birds there such as Clark's nutcracker, and mule deer, long-tailed weasels, and elk.

The upper limit of the subalpine ecosystem is at about 11,000 feet. Then there's a transition zone, where the same trees as found in the subalpine ecosystem exist, but in a smaller size. Finally you're there—the end of the world—where, at almost 12,000 feet elevation, the **alpine tundra** has no trees and many of its other plants are almost too tiny to see. The wildlife includes golden eagles, hawks, mice and other rodents, and yellow-bellied marmots, plus bighorn sheep and elk.

Old Fall River Road ends at Fall River Pass at the Alpine Visitor Center—watch for elk as you approach the visitor center. There it joins Trail Ridge Road, which you can take back to the east side of the park, or go west to cross the Continental Divide at Milner Pass and continue into the park's western section. Old Fall River Road is open to motor vehicles and mountain bikes; trailers and motor homes over 25 feet long are wisely prohibited.

**Stop No. 5: Forest Canyon Overlook.** From this stop's parking area, a short, paved walkway leads to an observation platform offering a beautiful but dizzying view into vast Forest Canyon, where the erosion work of glaciers is clearly evident, and a look at the peaks of the Continental Divide beyond. Near the overlook, watch for pikas (relatives of rabbits), marmots, and other small mammals. The elevation is 11,716 feet.

**Stop No. 6:** ✪ **Rock Cut.** Practically the highest point along Trail Ridge Road, this is the alpine tundra at its harshest, where winds can reach 150 miles per hour, winter blizzards are frequent, and temperatures in midsummer frequently drop below freezing. You'll have splendid views of the glacially carved peaks along the Continental Divide, and on the 0.5-mile **Tundra World Nature Trail** you'll find signs identifying and discussing the hardy plants and animals that inhabit this cold and barren region. The elevation is 12,110 feet.

**Stop No. 7: Lava Cliffs.** Here you'll see a dark cliff, created by the carving action of glacial ice through a thick layer of tuff (volcanic ash and debris) that was deposited here about 28 million years ago during volcanic eruptions in the Never Summer Range, located about 8 miles west. If you look just below the cliff, you'll see a pretty meadow that is a popular grazing spot of elk. The elevation is 12,080 feet.

**Stop No. 8: Fall River Pass.** At this spot you'll get a good view of a huge amphitheater, and you can take a break at the Alpine Visitor Center. A viewing platform at the rear of the visitor center offers views of a wide glacially carved valley of grasses, wildflowers, shrubs, and small trees where you're practically guaranteed to see elk grazing. This is also the junction of Trail Ridge Road and Old Fall River Road. The elevation is 11,796 feet.

**Stop No. 9: Medicine Bow Curve.** Views of a vast subalpine forest of spruce and fir and the distant Cache la Poudre River give way to the Medicine Bow Mountains, which extend into Wyoming. The elevation is 11,640 feet.

**Stop No. 10: Milner Pass.** This is the Continental Divide, the backbone of North America. From this point, water flows west to the Pacific or east toward the Atlantic. The divide also affects the park's weather—the west side is usually colder, is less windy, and receives much more precipitation than the east side. The elevation is 10,758 feet.

**Stop No. 11: Farview Curve.** This aptly named overlook provides a look at the beginnings of the Colorado River as it carves its way through the Kawuneeche Valley 1,000 feet below the overlook, before flowing some 1,400 miles to the Gulf of California. There are also panoramic views of the Never Summer Mountains, and looking west from this point you can see the Grand Ditch, which carries water across the Continental Divide to Colorado's thirsty eastern plains. Engelmann spruce and lodgepole pine grow here, and you'll see ground squirrels and chipmunks scurrying among the rocks. The elevation is 10,120 feet.

**Stop No. 12: Never Summer Ranch.** Just past the Timber Creek Campground, this stop provides access to a short trail to ✪ **Never Summer Ranch,** an early–20th-century home-stead that started out as a working cattle ranch, but soon evolved into a dude ranch. Rangers give talks and guided walks here during the summer. The elevation is 8,884 feet.

## 6  Ranger Programs & Guided Hikes

Various free ranger programs are offered throughout the year, although the greatest number and variety occur during the summer months. These include lectures on the park's wildlife, plants, geology, and human history. The programs may cover a very broad topic such as the living things that make their home in the park, or they may be a detailed analysis of sub-jects such as the role of ice in landscape development, or how beaver have changed the face of the park. Talks are held at the various visitor centers/museums, as well as at campground amphitheaters.

One of the best ways to explore the park, especially for the first-time visitor, is on a ranger-led walk or hike. These vary—based mostly on the interests and skills of the rangers on duty when you happen to visit—but might include strenuous hikes into the alpine tundra, a trek along the Continental Divide to look at different rock formations, or an easy nature walk. Rangers also lead photo walks, orienteering instruction trips, and wildlife-viewing walks. There are walks and talks at several of the park's historic sites, including Never Summer Ranch and the Moraine Park Museum.

At night, rangers periodically lead night-sky programs using the park's computerized telescopes, and offer nightly talks dur-ing the elk-rutting season each fall. Winter visitors will find a variety of activities, including ✪ **moonlight hikes,** snowshoe and cross-country ski trips, and Saturday-evening talks at the visitor centers. Consult the *High Country Headlines* newspaper (free at entrance stations and visitor centers) for scheduled activities during your visit.

## ESPECIALLY FOR KIDS

The park offers a variety of special hikes and programs for children, including an especially popular trip to the park's ✪ **beaver ponds.** A ranger-led program for kids from 6 to 12 years old, called **"A Child's View,"** concentrates on the park's geology and wildlife through hands-on activities. The park's ✪ **Junior Ranger Program** helps kids earn badges by completing activities that teach them about the park's plants and animals, and environmental concerns. Most of the kids' activities are scheduled during the summer; check on schedules at any park visitor center.

## 7  Historic Attractions

Although people believed to be the ancestors of today's American Indians lived in what is now Rocky Mountain National Park at least 12,000 years ago, they left little behind for present-day visitors to see. Lucky hikers with sharp eyes might see potsherds, pieces of ancient stone tools, and other archaeological objects. Near the tree line, watch for fire rings and the remains of rock game drives that are difficult to spot because they are simply lines of rocks. Park officials ask that you not touch any artifacts (skin oils can damage them), but report their location to rangers.

Most of these early peoples were hunters and gatherers who spent summers in the park, but wisely went to lower climes during the harsh winters. Arrowheads have been found from the Paleo-Indians, who hunted the woolly mammoth and other now-extinct animals between 9,500 and 7,000 B.C. There are also sites in the park attributed to the Archaic peoples, who occupied the area from 7,000 B.C. until about A.D. 100. They were followed by the Woodland peoples, believed to have lived in the area until about 1250, a view supported by pieces of pottery and other artifacts found in the park. In more modern times, members of the Ute and Arapaho tribes

## The Grand Ditch

For the pioneers and settlers who invaded the American West in the late 1800s and early 1900s, water was in many cases more precious than gold and silver. And so it was, in the 1880s, that work began on the creation of a channel to divert water from the Grand River (later renamed the Colorado River) on the west side of the Continental Divide, and to deliver it to thirsty farms east of the mountains.

Considered an engineering marvel at the time, the channel began sending water eastward in 1890 with 8 miles of ditch across a high mountain pass, dug by hand primarily by Japanese and Mexican laborers. By 1936, with the help of machinery, the ditch extended to 14.3 miles, leaving what some visitors consider an unsightly scar through the heart of Rocky Mountain National Park. First called the Grand River Ditch, it was renamed the Grand Ditch after the name of the Grand River was changed to the Colorado River in 1921.

Still in use today, the ditch is about 20 feet wide and 6 feet deep, although the water is usually no more than 3 feet deep. It runs east from Baker Creek, at an elevation of 10,300 feet, to La Poudre Pass, at an elevation of 10,175 feet, a grade of less than 0.2%. From Poudre Pass, water flows into a reservoir, then into the Cache la Poudre River, and finally to farmers and municipalities on the state's eastern plains near Fort Collins. However, the National Park Service has questioned the allocation of the water, and in recent years it has argued in court that the support of plant life, animal habitat, and other aspects of nature are just as valid as the needs of man for agriculture and drinking water.

An immediate effect of this water theft was a reduction in the fish population in the Colorado River. The water flow was cut in half, not only limiting the number of fish it could support, but also causing an increase in the water temperature, which further endangered the fish.

Hikers will get a close-up view of the ditch, whether they want it or not, along the Grand Ditch Trail, which also offers some pleasant scenic views. The Ditch is also clearly visible from the Coyote Valley Nature Trail, a few miles south. (See "West-Side Day Hikes," in chapter 4, for trail descriptions.)

are known to have hunted in the park, and their oral history tells of a number of conflicts between the tribes, presumably over hunting rights.

Remnants from the area's mining and ranching days of the late 1800s and early 1900s, as well as the beginnings of tourism, can be seen throughout the park. Hikers will encounter abandoned mines and the ruins of historic cabins on the Lulu City and Eugenia Mine trails (see chapter 4).

✪ **Lulu City,** supposedly named after the daughter of Benjamin Burnett, one of its founders, is one of the many western mining towns that sprang to life after the discovery of silver. After a brief heyday, the town collapsed into obscurity; today we might say that Lulu City had its 15 minutes of fame. The town was plotted in 1880 by miners Burnett and William Baker, and town lots measuring over 100 square blocks sold quickly, from $20 to $50 dollars each. Soon there were about 500 residents, regular mail and stage service, a fine hotel, a variety of stores, two sawmills, and a two-cabin red-light district.

But the town's ore was low-grade and there was no nearby smelter; by the fall of 1883 the town was practically deserted. As one of the regional newspapers said of Lulu City in early 1884, "The bears and mountain lions have taken possession. . . and are running a municipal government of their own." Today all that are left are several mines, tailings piles, cabin ruins, rusted pieces of mining equipment, and some wagon-wheel ruts—most of the town site has reverted to a delightful meadow that becomes a sea of wildflowers each summer.

The **Eugenia Mine** had an even less successful history. It was worked by Carl Norwall and his family in the early 1900s, and although Norwall enthusiastically dug more than 1,000 feet into Battle Mountain, no ore of any value was found. Curiously, though, Norwall was able to maintain a relatively elegant log home, complete with a piano, for himself, his wife, and their two daughters. Today, the remains of the cabin and discarded mining machines can be seen along the banks of a shallow brook, and the mine and tailings can be found several hundred feet upstream.

The **Moraine Park Museum,** on Bear Lake Road, contains exhibits mainly on natural history, but the handsome log building is listed on the National Register of Historic Places.

Constructed in 1923 from local ponderosa pine and glacial rocks, it was used as a social center, with a tearoom downstairs and dance hall upstairs. Nearby are several historic buildings—one dating from 1898—that are not open to the public.

A section of the **Fall River Store,** located next to the Alpine Visitor Center at Fall River Pass, was built in 1936 and provided an exhibit area, store, and rest rooms for Trail Ridge Road travelers. Two years later the building was enlarged to increase the size of the store and provide lodging for seasonal park employees. The original 1936 part of the building now houses the store's American Indian arts and crafts. Park employees no longer live in the building; those facilities have been converted to stockrooms, and the 1938 addition serves as the main gift shop. Another addition, done in 1965, contains a snack bar and dining area.

The ✪ **Never Summer Ranch,** a preserved dude ranch dating back to the 1920s, is an easy 0.5-mile walk from Trail Ridge Road on the west side of the park. It was started as a cattle ranch by Denver saloon owner John Holzwarth after Prohibition forced him to find a new line of work. But Holzwarth soon discovered that it was easier, and more profitable, to take in paying guests (at $2 per day or $11 per week, including room, meals, and a horse) than to do the hard work of actual ranching. Although the accommodations were rustic, even for that day, Sophie (Mama) Holzwarth's cooking—featuring local trout, deer, and grouse, along with traditional German dishes—made up for the primitive facilities. The ranch buildings contain many of their original furnishings, and visitors can see the bunkhouses, kitchens, a taxidermy shop, wagons, and sleds. Check at park visitor centers for times of guided tours and talks, offered during the summer.

Those looking for a historic or perhaps nostalgic experience should consider driving up **Old Fall River Road,** which is little changed from the day construction was completed in September 1920. See "Old Fall River Road: A Step Back in Time," above.

# 4

# Hikes & Other Outdoor Pursuits in Rocky Mountain National Park

*R*ocky Mountain National Park contains almost 350 miles of hiking trails, ranging from short, easy walks to extremely strenuous and challenging hikes that require climbing skills. The terrain ranges from paved paths to shady packed earth to rocky hillsides, and from level ground to unbelievably steep trails. Hiking difficulty can also vary according to the time of year—the higher elevations usually have snow until at least mid-July. Considering the park's reputation for rough terrain, it's a pleasant surprise to discover numerous easy and moderately rated trails that can be completed in a half day or less. Also, many park trails, such as Longs Peak, can be done either as day hikes or as overnight backpacking trips.

In planning your hikes, take into consideration the difference in elevation between where you live and where you plan to hike and camp. All trails in Rocky Mountain National Park begin above 7,000 feet and climb much higher. High-altitude sickness can put a damper on your vacation. If you live near sea level, it is recommended that you spend at least 1 night at 7,000 to 8,000 feet before hitting the trail. This will allow your body to begin adjusting to the environmental differences, particularly the decrease in oxygen. It can take several weeks to become fully acclimated. Hikers, especially those who plan to take on the longer and more strenuous trails, are strongly advised to discuss their plans with park rangers before setting out.

A number of trails in the adjacent national forests also provide good views of the park. For more information on the national forests, see chapter 6.

## 1 East-Side Day Hikes

With this area containing roughly two-thirds of the park's hiking trails, it's not surprising that you'll find the greatest variety of terrain here—both in length and in difficulty level. But it is also the busiest section of the park, and you are less likely to find the hiking solitude you may be seeking. Compared to trails on the west side of the park, trails here offer somewhat more spectacular scenery, with a dramatic snowcapped peak seemingly around every bend, and the terrain is a bit more open.

**Alberta Falls Trail.** 0.6 mile one-way. Easy. Access: Glacier Gorge Junction parking area, 8.5 miles down Bear Lake Rd.

With an elevation change of only 160 feet, this is an easy and scenic walk along Glacier Creek to pretty Alberta Falls. You'll cross the creek four times over wooden bridges. Along the trail you'll see beaver dams and an abundance of golden-mantled ground squirrels. For the first 0.25 mile the trail is smooth and level as it passes among fir, spruce, and aspen groves, which are especially colorful in the early fall. Then the trail gets a bit steeper, somewhat uneven, and sunnier, with views of the Mummy Mountain Range. From the falls—among the park's most impressive—you can turn around and walk back to the trailhead or continue to Mills Lake (see below). The starting elevation is 9,240 feet.

✪ **Bear Lake Nature Trail.** 0.5-mile loop. Easy. Access: Bear Lake Trailhead at the end of Bear Lake Rd.

Head out early in the day if you want some quiet time on this very popular walk. From the beginning of the trail, on the eastern side, 12,713-foot Hallett Peak dominates the view; along the lake's north side you'll be looking at the national park's highest mountain, 14,255-foot Longs Peak. Expect to see ground squirrels, chipmunks, and snowshoe hares, while in the clear waters of the lake you may catch a glimpse of a greenback cutthroat trout (sorry, no fishing is allowed). The Rocky Mountain Nature Association sells an informative booklet, *Bear Lake Nature Trail* ($2), at park visitor centers that makes a handy companion on your walk. This is an easy stroll, most of which is wheelchair accessible—one section has stairs. The elevation is 9,475 feet.

## Photography 101: Tips from a Pro

In photography, light is everything. Denver photographer Jack Olson, whose outdoor photography you've likely seen in books, magazines, and calendars, says, "A good photograph becomes a great photograph with the right light, and the best way to improve your photographs quickly is to teach yourself to recognize good light, and then to be at the right place at the right time."

Early and late in the day are the best times to take pictures, Olson says. "The sun is lower, the light has a warm color, good quality, and produces crisper shadows."

In contrast, light at midday is flat, and shadows are not as distinctive. "Just before sunrise to 1 hour after sunrise is magic time, and then 2 hours after is still good," he says. "Just the reverse is true in the evening—2 hours before sunset is okay, and then from 1 hour before sunset to just after is best."

Rocky Mountain National Park is among Olson's favorite shoots, he says, in part because Trail Ridge Road provides easy access to fantastic views. Still, he does much of his park photography from hiking trails, and he travels light, usually carrying one camera body and two lenses—a 35-millimeter wide angle and a 70- to 210-millimeter macro zoom. If he expects to see a lot of animals, he'll also pack a 400-millimeter telephoto, and for close quarters he sometimes uses a 28-millimeter.

Another essential item, even on a hike, is a sturdy tripod. Olson explains, "Most people who buy photographs want them sharp front to back—tack sharp they call it." He says that to get sharp photos you need good depth of field—the zone of

**Bierstadt Lake Trail.** 1.4 miles one-way. Moderate. Access: North side of Bear Lake Rd., 6.4 miles from Beaver Meadows.

This trail climbs 566 feet through an open and sunny forest of quaking aspen—especially pretty in fall—to Bierstadt Lake, where you will probably see mallards and other birds. There are boulders along the shore, and several beaches, although there are more stones here than sand. From the northwest side of the lake you'll have especially fine views of Longs Peak. This trail also connects with several other trails (watch the signs so you don't get lost), including one that leads to Bear Lake. The initial elevation is 8,850 feet.

sharp focus in front and behind the subject. For this you need a small lens opening, or *aperture*. Apertures are measured in f-stops, with the highest numbers having the smallest lens openings. However, the higher the f-stop the longer the lens must be open to produce a properly exposed photo. With his camera tripod-mounted, Olson sets the aperture to a high f-16 or f-22, which means that with the ISO 100 speed film he prefers, he usually must set the shutter speed at one-fifteenth or one-thirtieth of a second, which would surely produce a blurry shot if the camera were hand-held.

One exception to this tack-sharp rule, Olson says, is when he deliberately makes part of his photo blurry. "I like to shoot waterfalls and rushing streams, and very often I'll blur the action of the water to make it look like it's moving. But to do this you need a tripod because you're going to be shooting very slowly, perhaps one-fourth or one-eighth of a second."

Asked to divulge his secret spot for what he considers the finest scenery in the park, Olson says to wait until the snow-drifts have melted. Then, take a 28-millimeter wide-angle lens and head to Chasm Lake. "You go up above timberline, cross-ing a steep slope, with Longs Peak and Mount Meeker above you and this big valley below, with a little jewel of a pond—Peacock Pool. You've got a waterfall thundering down out of Chasm Lake, Longs Peak 2,000 feet above, and from that trail you get wonderful shots of Peacock Pool, or the waterfall and Longs Peak, or Chasm Lake and Longs Peak. It's exceptional, one of the most spectacular places in the park."

**Calypso Cascades Trail.** 1.8 miles one-way. Moderate. Access: Wild Basin Ranger Station.

This trail first takes you to Copeland Falls (see below) and then continues upward and onward through a subalpine for-est. For the first part of the hike, the trail follows the North St. Vrain Creek. You'll see Rocky Mountain maple, stumps of aspen cut down by beaver, wildflowers, and numerous birds. Continuing through a thick stand of lodgepole pine, you leave North St. Vrain Creek and follow Cony Creek as the trail becomes steeper, before arriving at the refreshing water-fall. The Calypso Cascades were named for the calypso, a purplish-pink member of the orchid family, also known as the fairy slipper. The starting elevation is 8,500 feet, and the trail has a 700-foot elevation gain.

**✪ Chasm Lake Trail.** 4.2 miles one-way. Strenuous. Access: Longs Peak Ranger Station.

This popular hike offers everything a hike should—trees, wildflowers, animals, a waterfall, a delightful lake, and a challenge that is rewarded by splendid views. The trail follows the East Longs Peak Trail (see below) for the first 3 miles, as you watch the trees get smaller and smaller until they disappear entirely at the tree line. After switchbacking up a moraine, you arrive at a trail junction, where you can go right to Longs Peak or left to Chasm Lake. Continuing toward the lake, you'll follow rock cairns in spots, with views of Longs Peak, before reaching Columbine Falls. Here you'll need to be especially careful as you follow a narrow ridge. After passing through a meadow of wildflowers, including Colorado blue columbine, and by a Park Service cabin, you'll climb to the top of another ridge until you finally arrive at Chasm Lake and its wonderful view of Longs Peak. The initial elevation is 9,300 feet, and the trail has a 2,390-foot elevation gain.

**✪ Copeland Falls Trail.** 0.3 mile one-way. Easy. Access: Wild Basin Ranger Station.

This pleasant walk along the North St. Vrain Creek can be among the park's most colorful. There's an abundance of wildflowers, such as wild rose, during the summer, and fall colors are supplied by an abundance of quaking aspen and Rocky Mountain maple, accented by the deep green of ponderosa pines. The trail leads to Copeland Falls, a small waterfall created by a sudden drop in the creek. Photographers will find that morning light is best for shooting the falls. The almost-flat trail rises 15 feet from its beginning elevation of 8,500 feet. From the falls you can turn around and head back to the trailhead, or you can continue on to Calypso Cascades (see above).

**Cub Lake Trail.** 2.3 miles one-way. Moderate. Access: Cub Lake Trailhead, from Bear Lake Rd. turn at Moraine Park and follow signs.

An excellent choice for hikers who want to see a wide variety of wildlife and wildflowers, this trail wanders through several different habitats over its relatively short distance. From the trailhead, you first cross a bridge over a branch of the Big Thompson River, passing beaver ponds and a marshy meadow under the shade of willows and thinleaf alder. As you continue, you'll see evidence of browsing by elk and, if the season's right, a tremendous variety of wildflowers, including shooting stars and chimingbells. The trail passes through a wood of Douglas fir and ponderosa pine and fields of glacially carved boulders, where you might glimpse yellow-bellied marmots. There's a relatively steep but shady climb, and suddenly you're at Cub Lake, where you'll likely be greeted by ducks. In summer the lake is usually covered with yellow pond lilies, which produce a wonderful foreground for a photo of 12,922-foot Stones Peak, best shot from the lake's eastern shore. The starting elevation is 8,080 feet, and the trail has an elevation gain of 540 feet.

**Deer Mountain Trail.** 3 miles one-way. Strenuous. Access: Deer Ridge Junction, at the intersection of U.S. Highways 34 and 36, just under 3 miles northwest of the Beaver Meadows Entrance Station.

Panoramic views of Longs Peak, Ypsilon Mountain, and the entire eastern side of the park are your reward on this hike, which is really strenuous only at the very end, as you make the final ascent to the top of Deer Mountain. It is, however, sunny and dry, so make sure you carry plenty of water. Because the upper elevations of this trail are a favorite target for lightning strikes, it's best to start hiking early in the day so you're off the mountain by the time the usual afternoon summer thunderstorms roll in.

The trail begins with a walk along a sunny slope near ponderosa pines. At a junction you'll bear right, passing a wide variety of delightful wildflowers, before entering a grove of quaking aspen that bear numerous scars caused by hungry elk in winter. There are a number of switchbacks along the trail, which lead to a flat shoulder, where you'll see the dramatic results of fires caused by lightning strikes. The trail leads to a spur to the right, where it seems to head straight up to the summit. The trail starts at 8,930 feet and gains 1,083 feet in elevation.

✪ **East Longs Peak Trail.** 8 miles one-way. Very strenuous. Access: Longs Peak Ranger Station.

This challenging trail—recommended only for experienced mountain hikers and climbers in top physical condition—

climbs about 4,855 feet from a trailhead elevation of 9,400 feet to the top of 14,255-foot Longs Peak, the highest point in the park. The trek takes most hikers 13 to 15 hours to complete (7 or 8 hours up, an hour or so at the summit, and 5 or 6 hours down) and can be done in either 1 or 2 days. Those planning a 1-day hike should consider starting out at 2 or 3am so they will be off the peak well before the summer afternoon thunderstorms arrive. For a 2-day hike, go 5 or 6 miles the first day, stay at a designated backcountry campsite, and complete the trip the following day. The trail usually requires technical climbing gear until about mid-July, and until that time hikers should also be prepared for icy conditions.

The hike follows the Chasm Lake Trail (see above) for the first 3 miles, to an intersection on Mills Moraine, where you'll make a right turn. Here you pass Jims Grove, with views of 13,281-foot Mount Lady Washington. The grove was named for local mountain man, guide, and general character Jim Nugent, who lived in the area from the 1860s until his murder in 1874. From Jims Grove it's about 0.7 miles to Granite Pass, which is some 2,600 feet above the trailhead. Here, hikers choose the left fork of a junction, head up some steep switchbacks, and eventually get to the Boulder Field (2 miles from Granite Pass), where nine backcountry campsites are tucked among immense boulders beneath the north face of Longs Peak. From the Boulder Field it's a demanding 0.5-mile hike to the Keyhole, an appropriately named oval notch between Longs Peak and Storm Peak that offers spectacular views of the mountains.

Red and yellow signs mark the trail from the Keyhole to the summit. It's a distance of only 1.5 miles, but when you add in an elevation gain of 1,200 feet over extremely rough terrain, and the lack of oxygen at this altitude, you'll need to allow at least 2 hours for the hike. This part of the trek initially follows an exposed ledge and then goes through a steep stone-filled gully before reaching the Narrows, a skinny ledge that runs for several hundred feet along a steep drop-off. From there, hikers become climbers to ascend a steep granite incline called Homestretch, taking them to the summit, where they'll savor what many consider the best view in the park, as well as a well-deserved feeling of accomplishment.

# Longs Peak & Wild Basin Trails

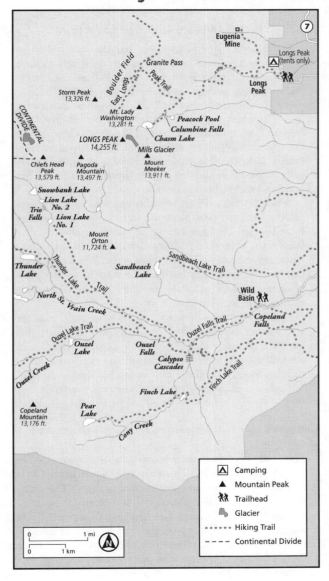

---

### Rocky's Ultimate Challenge: Longs Peak

Longs Peak was a landmark for the Utes, Arapahos, and earlier people who traveled, hunted, and sometimes fought in these mountains, and it is believed that ancient Indians scaled Longs Peak's summit, perhaps in efforts to trap eagles. The first recorded sighting of Longs Peak by white Americans occurred in 1820, when a 19-man army expedition led by Major Stephen Long, a member of the Army Engineers Corps, saw it. On a mission to find the source of the Platte River, the party saw the mountain that would later bear Long's name, but initially mistook it for another great landmark, Pikes Peak. They noted its location, but did not attempt to climb it.

When American settlers began moving into the area several decades later, the peak presented an obvious challenge, and some believed the mountain to be insurmountable. After a failed attempt in 1864, William Byers, editor of the Denver newspaper the *Rocky Mountain News,* wrote, "We are quite sure that no living creature, unless it had wings to fly, was ever upon its summit, and we believe we run no risk in predicting that no man ever will be."

Byers proved himself wrong just 4 years later when he accompanied a group led by John Wesley Powell, a one-armed Civil War veteran, geologist, and seemingly fearless explorer, on a trip all the way to the top. The expedition members reported that they found no evidence that anyone had been to the summit before them, and Byers wrote, "The peak is a nearly level

---

✪ **Emerald Lake Trail.** 1.8 miles one-way. Easy to moderate. Access: Bear Lake Trailhead.

This trail offers spectacular scenery on its route past Nymph and Dream lakes to its destination of Emerald Lake. The 0.5-mile hike to Nymph Lake is easy, climbing only 225 feet; from then on, the trail is rated moderate as it heads to Dream Lake (another 0.6 miles) and to Emerald Lake (another 0.7 miles), which is 605 feet higher than the starting point at Bear Lake. In addition to the mountain lakes, the views of the surrounding mountains are especially pretty when reflected in the surface of Nymph Lake, or when towering over Dream Lake. You walk among lodgepole and limber pines and fir, and in

surface, paved with irregular blocks of granite, and without any vegetation of any kind, except a little gray lichen."

More climbers followed, including an Englishwoman, Isabella Bird. One of the first women to reach the summit, she made the ascent with local guide Jim Nugent in the fall of 1873, and later wrote to her sister: "Had I known that the ascent was a real mountaineering feat, I should not have felt the slightest ambition to perform it. As it is, I am only humiliated by my success, for Jim dragged me up, like a bale of goods, by sheer force of muscle." A local minister began taking hikers to the top of Longs Peak in 1878 for $5 per person, and the first recorded winter climb was made by naturalist Enos Mills in 1903.

Although hiking and climbing to the top of Longs Peak soon became relatively common, it remained—and still remains—a hazardous expedition. Just before hikers get to the Keyhole, they come upon a stone hut with a bronze tablet that memorializes Agnes Vaille and Herbert Sortland, who died in January 1925. Vaille and another climber are credited with being the first to make a winter ascent along the peak's east face, but the trip exhausted her so much that she could climb only partway down and had frozen to death before a rescue party could reach her. Sortland, a member of that rescue party, had turned back, but became lost, fell and broke a hip, and died of exposure. More than 60 people have perished in attempts to scale Longs Peak.

summer there's an abundance of wildflowers along the path between Nymph and Dream lakes. The starting elevation is 9,475 feet.

**Eugenia Mine Trail.** 1.4 miles one-way. Moderate. Access: Longs Peak Ranger Station.

This walk to an abandoned mine follows the Longs Peak Trail for about a half mile and then forks off to the right. It heads through groves of aspens and then evergreens before arriving at the site of the mine, where you'll see hillside tailings, the remnants of a cabin, and abandoned mine equipment. The trail gains 508 feet in elevation from its starting point at 9,400 feet.

✪ **Fern Lake Trail.** 3.8 miles one-way. Moderate. Access: Fern Lake Trailhead, from Bear Lake Rd. turn west at Moraine Park and follow signs past the Cub Lake Trailhead.

This trail provides a variety of experiences for hikers. The first 1.5 miles follow a wide, relatively flat trail through ferns, Rocky Mountain maples, and aspen, roughly paralleling the Big Thompson River, whose banks are lined with narrowleaf cottonwood, water birch, and thinleaf alder. In the fall, the shades of yellow and red provide a colorful background. Kids can climb the boulders strewn along the trail and watch for evidence of beavers along the river.

Arch Rocks consist of several boulders that form an arch overhead—they are best seen from the other side, so turn around after you walk under. These rock monoliths are believed to have fallen from the cliffs above after the glaciers receded, although one huge hunk came crashing down nearby in the winter of 1992/93. If you're here near dusk, watch for beaver, that seem to prefer working after dark.

Now the trail heads uphill to The Pool, located downstream from the meeting of the Fern and Spruce creeks with the Big Thompson River. The force of the water as it flows between steep stone walls has carved a shallow pool, and the flat rocks around The Pool make great picnic spots. Cross the log bridge over the Big Thompson and take the path straight ahead (the left fork heads to Cub Lake; see above). You'll soon begin climbing along the side of a gully to enter a thick wood before crossing Fern Creek. Then, as you climb a ridge, your ears are bombarded by the noise of Spruce Creek on your right and Fern Creek on your left as they tumble down the mountainside. In July the unusual clustered lady's-slipper blooms along the trail here, rather low to the ground.

About a mile from The Pool and 480 feet higher, you'll reach Fern Falls, in a dense wood of Engelmann spruce and fir. It's prettiest around midday when the sunlight filters through the trees. Next the trail inclines steeply upward for another mile toward Fern Lake. As you cross the creek at its outlet from the lake, and pass out of the trees onto the shore, you see Notchtop Mountain and the Little Matterhorn rising majestically beyond the forest across the lake. Turn to your right and you can see Stones Peak in the distance. The beginning elevation is 8,155 feet, and the rise to Fern Lake is 1,375 feet.

**Impressions**

*You can't see anything from your car. You've got to get out of the damn thing and walk!*

—author Edward Abbey

**Finch Lake Trail.** 4.5 miles one-way. Moderate. Access: Finch Lake Trailhead, from the Wild Basin Ranger Station, 1,000 ft. east of the bridge over N. St. Vrain Creek; sign on south side of road.

The trail heads east and uphill from the road before doubling back on itself to head west on level ground for a bit through lodgepole pines and aspens. Stay to the right at the first intersection, continuing through aspens and climbing along wide switchbacks. As you pause for breath, look to the north across Wild Basin to see, left to right, Chiefs Head, Pagoda Mountain, and Mount Meeker. A slow downhill grade brings you to Confusion Junction, a three-way intersection that for some unknown reason seems to disorient many hikers. Take the middle path and you'll be just fine. You'll now follow a gradual incline along the northwest flank of Meadow Mountain, crossing a fire corridor and several streams before going over a small ridge and finally descending to Finch Lake. The calm waters often display fine reflections of Copeland Mountain, located due west. The initial elevation is 8,470 feet, and there is a gain of 1,442 feet.

**Flattop Mountain Trail.** 4.4 miles one-way. Strenuous. Access: Bear Lake Trailhead.

Follow the trail around the north side of Bear Lake (signs will keep you on the right track); eventually you will take a left-hand switchback away from Bierstadt Lake Trail and head uphill toward Flattop. As you climb the south-facing slope above Bear Lake, you approach an area that was burned out in 1900 and is finally being reforested with Engelmann spruce and subalpine firs. The next left fork (the right heads to Odessa Lake; see below) continues the uphill trek through the trees to an overlook for Dream Lake. This stop affords grand views of Glacier Gorge and Longs Peak to the south, and a closer view of Hallett Peak to the west. As you climb above the tree line, there's an overlook for Emerald Lake before the final 1.5-mile climb up a steep incline to the top of Flattop

Mountain. Take your time to enjoy the increasingly fine views of Hallett, now to your south. As its name implies, Flattop boasts a wide, somewhat smooth flat area at its summit, rather than a defined peak. The starting elevation for this trail is 9,475 feet, and the elevation gain is 2,849 feet.

**Gem Lake Trail.** 1.8 miles one-way. Moderate. Access: Twin Owls Trailhead. Or 2 miles one-way. Moderate. Access: Gem Lake Trailhead. Both trailheads are off Devil's Gulch Rd., north of Estes Park. Twin Owls Trailhead is inside Mac-Gregor Ranch (turn in at the ranch and go 0.8 miles to the end of the road). Gem Lake Trailhead is 0.75 miles past the turnoff into the ranch, at a parking lot on the left side of the road. The first 0.5 mile here is through private land.

This is a relatively low elevation trail, meandering across an open south-facing slope dotted with ponderosa pine. It can be quite warm on a sunny day, so take plenty of water. There are great views of Estes Park and Longs Peak to the south, particularly in early-morning and late-afternoon light. Lumpy Ridge bounds the trail on the north, with interesting and sometimes funny rock formations. The only limit to what you'll see is your imagination—many people discern Gila monsters and chickens, and in one odd heap, two turtles piled atop a whale! Eventually the trail brings you to tiny Gem Lake, covering only 0.2 acres and just 1 to 5 feet deep! It may seem unimpressive at first, but rest here a bit and you might catch a glimpse of white-throated swifts, rarely seen elsewhere in the park, soaring above the lake. Limber pines and Douglas fir dot the shoreline, and at the water's far end, you can get a picture-perfect view of the lake, framed by evergreens and topped with majestic mountains. The starting elevation at Gem Lake Trailhead is 7,740 feet, and there is an elevation increase of 1,090 feet as you hike to the lake; Twin Owls Trailhead is at 7,920 feet elevation, so the elevation gain is only 910 feet.

✪ **Lake Haiyaha Trail.** 2.1 miles one-way. Moderate. Access: Bear Lake Trailhead.

The first mile of this hike is along the trail to Dream Lake (described under "Emerald Lake Trail," above), but just before you reach Dream Lake, the Lake Haiyaha trail takes a left, crossing Tyndall Creek. As you head up the trail, look to your right for a pretty view of Dream Lake, and notice, if there are other hikers there, how well voices carry in these natural amphitheaters. As the trail winds up and around, different vistas open up. At one point, you will have a distant view of Estes Park, then Nymph and Bear lakes appear in the valleys below, and even Sprague Lake can be glimpsed farther down Bear Lake Road. To the southeast are grand views of Longs Peak soaring above Mills Lake. Shortly before reaching Lake Haiyaha, the trail to The Loch and Mills Lake takes off southward. Next you will pass a lovely little pond with boulders dotted along its shores. There is a hint of a trail ahead, which becomes ever more rocky, until finally you reach Lake Haiyaha, resting serenely in a huge bed of boulders. Those who don't mind scrambling over the rocks to the opposite side of the lake will be rewarded with a neatly framed view of Longs Peak. The initial elevation is 9,475 feet, and the elevation gain is 745 feet.

**Lawn Lake Trail.** 6.2 miles one-way. Strenuous. Access: Lawn Lake Trailhead on Fall River Rd.

This hike follows the Roaring River through terrain dotted with ponderosa pine. Along the way you can see all too plainly the damage done by a massive flood that occurred when a dam, which has since been removed, broke in 1982, killing three campers. At the higher elevations, there are scenic views of Mummy Mountain. The trail begins at an elevation of 8,540 feet and climbs another 2,249 feet.

✪ **The Loch Trail.** 2.7 miles one-way. Moderate. Access: Glacier Gorge Junction parking area, 8.5 miles down Bear Lake Rd.

From the Glacier Gorge Junction trailhead, continue past Alberta Falls (see above) and the junction for Mills Lake Trail (see below). Take plenty of water and sunscreen because this trail alternates between lovely forests and open slopes. Panoramic views will capture your attention while you're on the open slopes, and, on the rest of the trail, close-ups of wildflowers, aspen, and limber pine will draw your focus. Close to the lake you'll find patches of snow well into summer, and who among us can resist the temptation of pitching snowballs in July?

The rocky shoreline of The Loch is dotted with striking limber pines, and tall mountains frame the scene. The sheer Cathedral Wall, popular with rock climbers, dominates the western side. From the northeastern end of The Loch, gaze across the lake to Timberline Falls (see below), over a mile away. Above the falls is Taylor Peak, with a small glacier cling-ing to its left side. From some vantage points the larger Andrews Glacier, on the north flank of Taylor Peak, can be observed. Take the trail around the lake to find a private nook for a picnic if the popular northern shore is too crowded. The beginning elevation is 9,240 feet, and the elevation gain is 940 feet.

**Mills Lake Trail.** 2.5 miles one-way. Moderate. Access: Glacier Gorge Junction parking area, 8.5 miles down Bear Lake Rd.

This trail leads to a picturesque mountain lake, nestled in a valley among towering mountain peaks. The lake was named for Enos Mills, a naturalist who believed in protecting the wilderness for the refreshment of the soul, and who worked unceasingly for the establishment of Rocky Mountain National Park. Among the best spots in the park for photographing dra-matic Longs Peak (the best lighting is usually in late afternoon or early evening), this is also the perfect place for a picnic. Mornings, when the lake is still, are the best time to observe the reflections of shoreline rocks and trees in the water. The starting elevation is 9,240 feet, and the trail climbs only about 700 feet more.

**Moraine Park Interpretative Trail.** 0.5-mile loop. Easy; wheelchair-accessible with assistance. Access: Moraine Park Museum.

This nature trail winds through the meadow surrounding the museum, with five interpretive stops, and benches strategically positioned to take best advantage of the scenic views. It's a good idea to explore the museum before walking the trail, to better understand some of the things you'll be seeing. The first stop, in front of the museum, allows you to observe the geol-ogy of Moraine Park and how glaciers formed it, depositing the rocks and boulders you see strewn about. Stop no. 2 asks you to imagine the glacier that inhabited this moraine some 18,000 years ago—a mound over 1,000 feet high covering the entire valley before you, and pushing rocky debris ahead of it as it came down from the mountains above. From here you can see several glaciers in the distance: Taylor Glacier rests in a protected bowl on the southeast face of Taylor Peak; Andrews Glacier clings to the northwest flank of Taylor Peak; Tyndall Glacier lies between Hallett Peak and Flattop Moun-tain; and Sprague Glacier appears to be hanging below

# Bear Lake & Moraine Park Trails

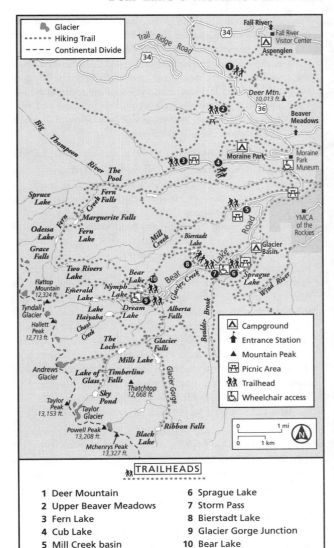

**Map Legend:**
- Glacier
- ····· Hiking Trail
- – – – Continental Divide

Trail Ridge Road
34
Fall River
Fall River Visitor Center
Aspenglen
Deer Mtn. 10,013 ft. ▲
36
Beaver Meadows
Big Thompson River
The Pool
Fern Creek Falls
Spruce Lake
Marguerite Falls
Odessa Lake
Fern Lake
Grace Falls
Two Rivers Lake
Flattop Mountain 12,324 ft.
Emerald Lake
Tyndall Glacier
Hallett Peak 12,713 ft.
Lake Haiyaha
Chaos Creek
The Loch
Andrews Glacier
Lake of Glass
Timberline Falls
Mills Lake
Sky Pond
Taylor Peak 13,153 ft.
Taylor Glacier
Powell Peak 13,208 ft.
Mchenrys Peak 13,327 ft.
Black Lake
Ribbon Falls
Thatchtop 12,668 ft.
Glacier Gorge
Glacier Falls
Alberta Falls
Dream Lake
Nymph Lake
Bear Lake
Bierstadt Lake
Mill Creek
Bear Lake
Glacier Creek
Boulder Brook
Sprague Lake
Glacier Basin
YMCA of the Rockies
Wind River
Bear Lake Road
Moraine Park
Moraine Park Museum

**Map Symbols:**
- ▲ Campground
- ♦ Entrance Station
- ▲ Mountain Peak
- 🏕 Picnic Area
- 🚶 Trailhead
- ♿ Wheelchair access

Scale: 0 — 1 mi / 0 — 1 km

## 🚶 TRAILHEADS

1 Deer Mountain
2 Upper Beaver Meadows
3 Fern Lake
4 Cub Lake
5 Mill Creek basin
6 Sprague Lake
7 Storm Pass
8 Bierstadt Lake
9 Glacier Gorge Junction
10 Bear Lake

Sprague Mountain. Stop no. 3 describes the role of the weather in everyone's experience in Rocky Mountain National Park. Stop no. 4 discusses several of the park's plants and animals, such as the majestic ponderosa pines that are scattered about the meadow, the elk and mule deer that frequent Moraine Park seeking food and water, and the striking mountain bluebird. The fifth stop finally gets around to humans and their impact on the area now known as Rocky Mountain National Park. The elevation here is 8,125 feet.

**Odessa Lake Trail.** 4.1 miles one-way. Moderate. Access: Bear Lake Trailhead.

Head right around Bear Lake, following the trail toward Flattop Mountain (see above), but at the second junction take the right fork. From here the trail is relatively level, with gentle ups and downs for about 2 miles, until you find yourself at Odessa Gorge. Soon the trail turns northeast around Joe Mills Mountain, traversing the side of the gorge and providing views of Grace Falls on the opposite wall. Until mid-July you'll likely be crossing snowbanks and ice in this area, which can make the hike very treacherous. At the next junction, turn left (the right fork takes you to Fern Lake) and follow Fern Creek upstream to Odessa Lake. Notchtop Mountain and the Little Matterhorn rise majestically south of the lake. The beginning elevation is 9,475 feet and you'll gain 1,205 feet in elevation when you head to Odessa Lake. If you want a longer hike, return to the junction and head left toward Fern Lake (elevation drop of 1,150 ft.), then continue down to Moraine Park (elevation drop of 1,450 ft.), for a total hike of 9.6 miles. Take the Bear Lake Shuttle to get back to your car.

**Old Ute Trail.** 6 miles one-way. Moderate. Access: Old Ute Trail turnout (also called Ute Crossing) on Trail Ridge Rd., 2 miles west of Rainbow Curve.

An excellent way to see the tundra, this hike is really fairly easy if you arrange a ride to the top (there are no shuttle buses or ride-arranging bulletin boards or services; make arrangements on your own with friends) and walk down to Upper Beaver Meadows.

As you leave Trail Ridge Road, the incline is gentle and marked by rock cairns. Forest Canyon lies below to your right, with the Big Thompson River flowing through it, and the Continental Divide marks the horizon beyond. As you round a bend, the road is blocked from sight, allowing you to imagine what the Utes and Arapaho faced when they followed this trail in years past. Longs Peak can be seen to the south; the clear air gives the illusion you can almost reach out and touch it, but it's actually 10 miles away! As you head for Tombstone Ridge, you may see yellow-bellied marmots relaxing on rocks in the sun, or pikas scurrying about gathering their winter fodder. In early morning you may catch a glimpse of deer or elk grazing on the tundra. From the top of Tombstone Ridge, the Mummy Range dominates the northern skyline, and Trail Ridge Road winds its way below.

You will next descend below the tree line among limber pines and into Windy Gulch. This hanging valley is midway between the top of Trail Ridge and the bottom of Forest Canyon; it was created by drainage from the ridge but left hanging above the canyon dug by a narrow glacier thousands of years ago. The Windy Gulch Cascades are where the drainage stream tumbles off the edge of the gulch, down the steep, almost clifflike, wall and into the Big Thompson River. When you reach this point, you'll have terrific views of Notchtop, Gabletop, and Knobtop mountains, with Mount Wuh (10,761 ft.) blocking farther views to the south. Longs Peak dominates the view to the southeast. The trail now bends around Beaver Mountain to the northeast, through forests of ponderosa pine, aspen, juniper, and Douglas fir, on its final descent to Upper Beaver Meadows. The trail's starting point is at 11,440 feet. The elevation gain to Tombstone Ridge is 160 feet; the drop to Upper Beaver Meadows is about 3,000 feet.

✪ **Ouzel Falls Trail.** 2.7 miles one-way. Moderate. Access: Wild Basin Ranger Station.

This hike takes you past Copeland Falls (see above), crosses Cony Creek, and heads west at Calypso Cascades (see above) before beginning a series of switchbacks up to Ouzel Falls. Look to the trees to the north for some wonderful views of Mount Meeker and Longs Peak. This part of the trail takes you through areas that were burned in a 1978 fire but are now peppered with lovely wildflowers, flitting butterflies, and grazing wildlife. As you climb through the rocks, the delightful sound of tumbling water draws you forward. Suddenly you're there—gazing up at one of the loveliest waterfalls in the park. The best view is from the rocks on the south side, located just before the bridge that crosses the creek, but scramble onto them carefully as they are very slippery. Look for the chunky brown water ouzel, or American dipper, for whom the falls are named—they dart into the water and behind the falls seeking food. The initial elevation is 8,500 feet, and the elevation gain is 950 feet.

**Sandbeach Lake Trail.** 4.2 miles one-way. Strenuous. Access: Sandbeach Lake Trailhead at the east end of the road into Wild Basin Ranger Station, near Copeland Lake.

It's good to know there's a reward at the end of this challenging hike. From the trailhead, it's a little over a mile of steep climbing through the woods up Copeland Moraine. The ridge is achieved after several short switchbacks, and the trail from Meeker Park joins from the right. About another mile of climbing brings you to Campers Creek crossing. From there it's another mile to Hunters Creek crossing, and the final mile of the climb brings you to one of the prettiest lakes in the park, with an attractive beach and striking mountains in the distance. The beginning elevation is 8,312 feet, and the elevation gain is 1,971 feet.

✪ **Sprague Lake Nature Trail.** 0.5-mile loop. Easy. Access: Sprague Lake parking area, 5.7 miles down Bear Lake Rd.

This wheelchair-accessible trail follows the shoreline of Sprague Lake. The short guide to the trail ($1, available at park visitor centers) describes the area's history, flora, and fauna and names the grand array of peaks seen from the far side of the lake. On still days, the reflections in the water are spectacular.

The trail wanders among lodgepole pines on the east, providing numerous opportunities to see chipmunks and ground squirrels scurrying about, mallards paddling among the reeds and marshes where they nest in early spring, and a myriad of insects feeding in and around the water. Several railed wooden platforms are built over the water, from which youngsters can peer into the lake trying to spot cutthroat trout or a frog, and benches are strategically placed along the trail for resting and absorbing the view. Several are located about halfway around, where the views of the peaks are best. This area also has large boulders, great for climbing, perching upon, and picnicking. As you look out over the lake to the western peaks, you can see Tyndall Glacier almost forming a bridge between Hallett Peak and Flattop Mountain. The lake is shallow—only about 9 feet deep—and freezes over quite early in the fall, but it's still a lovely place to walk and even picnic on a sunny day. Boardwalks and bridges have been built over the marshy western side of the lake, to take you back to the trailhead. The elevation is 8,710 feet.

**Timberline Falls Trail.** 4 miles one-way. Strenuous. Access: Glacier Gorge Junction parking area, 8.5 miles down Bear Lake Rd.

Follow the hike to The Loch (see above) and continue around the shady path on the lake's northwest side. The trail follows Icy Brook for just under a mile after The Loch. When you reach a fork in the trail, stay to the left for 0.25 miles to reach the catch basin of Timberline Falls. This beautiful open area is dotted with boulders on which you can rest while absorbing the sight and rushing sound of the three-tiered waterfall. This part of the trail climbs 1,210 feet above its initial elevation of 9,240 feet.

For those with time and energy, the trail continues up beside the waterfall, and over the slippery rocks—which can be icy in early summer—until you are above the tree line, as the waterfall's name indicates. A 0.2-mile climb over bedrock will bring you to the Lake of Glass and its wondrous views of The Loch and the magnificent peaks beyond. Perched among the rocks and the tundra, the Lake of Glass displays a barren beauty. Continue around the lake another 0.4 miles to the larger and even more desolate Sky Pond, below the east face of Taylor Peak. It's cold and windy here most of the time, but take your time heading down to enjoy the changing panoramic views. From Timberline Falls, the elevation increase to Sky Pond is 450 feet.

**Tundra World Nature Trail.** 0.5-mile loop. Easy. Access: Near Rock Cut Parking Area on Trail Ridge Rd.

This wheelchair-accessible nature trail is an excellent quick introduction to the alpine tundra, with exhibits identifying the tundra plants and animals, and describing how they have adapted to the harsh environment. The elevation is 12,110 feet.

**Twin Sisters Peak Trail.** 3.4 miles one-way. Strenuous. Access: Twin Sisters Trailhead at the Lily Lake Visitor Center on the east side of Colo. 7.

Most of this trail seems to go straight up, and you'll be utilizing numerous switchbacks as you cross the park boundary.

About 2.2 miles from the trailhead you'll come out onto a ridge north of the summit. Lookout Springs is about 0.25 miles east of the trail, but because the water here is questionable, it's best to carry your own. The trail becomes rockier and even steeper as you approach the timberline, so take a breather and admire the panoramic peaks to the west. The early-morning sun, for those who started well before sunrise, defines the peaks clearly and dramatically against the sky.

Directly across the valley is the impressive East Face of Longs Peak. On top, the views are fantastic in all directions. Camping is not permitted on Twin Sisters, but for those with sufficient stamina, an evening hike by moonlight can be memorable. A fire lookout tower was removed from Twin Sisters in 1977 after it was deemed ineffective, and there is now a radio repeater lodged in a hut atop the peak. The trail starts at an elevation of 9,040 feet and ascends 2,388 feet.

## 2  West-Side Day Hikes

You will not have as many trail choices on this side of the park as you do on the east side, but you'll be sharing those trails with far fewer humans; and your chances of seeing wildlife will be better. Because the west side of the park gets more precipitation than the east, there are more plants, with thicker foliage here. Views are not quite as dramatic as those from the park's east-side trails, but they're still well worth the effort. It's also usually cooler on this side of the park.

**Big Meadows Trail.** 1.8 miles one-way. Easy to moderate. Access: Green Mountain Trailhead, 3.2 miles north of the Grand Lake Entrance Station.

Follow an old wagon road through a subalpine forest to the ruins of a ranch on this trail. The path is wide and smooth, and, near dusk and dawn, hikers are often rewarded with sightings of deer and elk. Most of the trail follows a brook, along which wild blueberries and occasionally wild strawberries can be found. The gentle incline leads to Big Meadows, a large and open field as the name implies, where wildflowers are tucked among the grasses. Look for the unusual pink elephant heads, whose flowers resemble miniature elephant heads with upturned trunk and floppy ears; or cinquefoil, a member of the rose family used by early peoples to treat ailments such as toothaches, fevers, and infections. The remnants of Sam Stone's log cabin and barn give stark evidence of

# Colorado River Trails

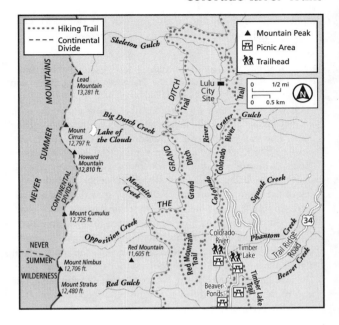

his attempt at ranching here in the early 1900s. The beginning elevation is 8,794 feet, and the elevation gain is 606 feet.

**Cascade Falls Trail.** 3.5 miles one-way. Moderate. Access: Tonahutu/North Inlet Trailhead off Colo. 278 on the north side of downtown Grand Lake, at the east end of the parking area.

Stroll the first 1.2 miles of this hike on relatively flat, private ranch lands, where cows and horses graze, before entering park property and reaching Summerland Park, a favorite picnicking and family-camping spot. Continue on the trail as it moves through stands of aspen and lodgepole pines, rising gently into forests of Engelmann spruce and subalpine fir. As you climb, mountain walls draw closer, providing beautiful views of the rock cliffs, and the moss resulting from the more frequent rains on this side of the park. Wildflowers often grace the trail's edges. As you approach the tumultuous falls, the increasing noise level prohibits conversation. The trail separates into two paths below the falls, each climbing around to the top. It's best to take the lower, right fork up and to come down on the other path, thereby avoiding confrontations with equestrians. The falls lie to the right of the right fork. The hike's initial elevation is 8,540 feet, and there is an elevation gain of 300 feet.

✪ **Coyote Valley Nature Trail.** 1-mile loop. Easy. Access: On the west side of Trail Ridge Rd., 5.4 miles north of the Grand Lake Entrance Station and 2.3 miles south of Timber Creek Campground.

This wheelchair- and stroller-accessible trail is a delight, with numerous benches and interpretive signs scattered along the path. The trail parallels the Colorado River as it wends its way through the Kawuneeche Valley. Prior to the establishment of Rocky Mountain National Park, researchers discovered that the Arapaho had named this valley *Kawuneeche,* meaning "valley of the coyotes." You can occasionally spot the doglike animal slipping through the meadows seeking rodents and other prey. Many of the plants the Arapaho used for food and medicine can still be found in this valley, and so can the lodgepole pines they used for teepee poles. As you walk the trail, look at the Grand Ditch (see "Historic Attractions," in chapter 3) on the east-facing slopes of the Never Summer Mountains. The end of the trail loops through a stand of lodgepole pines. The elevation is 8,766 feet.

**East Inlet Trail.** 6.9 miles one-way. Moderate to strenuous. Access: The west portal of Adam's Tunnel, southeast of the town of Grand Lake.

This trail is an easy walk for the first 0.3 miles to scenic Adams Falls, where early-morning hikers are frequently blessed with a rainbow sparkling through the rising mist. The trail then wanders through meadows—sometimes marshy and mosquito-ridden—as it follows the East Inlet, one of the two tributaries of Grand Lake. Spur trails lead to the banks of the river, where you may find evidence of beaver if you look closely—both dams and lodges can be seen in East Meadow. As you hike, glance occasionally at the domineering sight of Mount Craig, or Mount Baldy as it is commonly called in Grand Lake because of its treeless rounded peak.

After East Meadow, the trail begins to climb sharply toward Lone Pine Lake, about 5.5 miles from the trailhead. From the switchbacks along here you can occasionally see Mount Craig off to the south. Lone Pine Lake was named for the single lodgepole pine that once took root on the rock island in the middle of the lake. It has since been replaced by several pines and an Engelmann spruce. The trail continues along the southern shoreline of the lake before the final climb to Lake Verna. Passing among trees and rocks, crossing long bridges over brooks streaming down Andrews Peak to the north, and wandering again through a subalpine forest, the trail finally emerges onto a rocky ridge overlooking Lake Verna. This vista allows you to appreciate the fjordlike design of this lovely lake. The trail continues on past the lake, but it is not maintained. The starting elevation is 8,391 feet, and the total elevation gain to Lake Verna is 1,809 feet.

**Grand Ditch Trail.** 3.4 miles one-way. Strenuous. Access: Colorado River Trailhead on the west side of Trail Ridge Rd., 9.6 miles north of the Grand Lake Entrance Station.

Head north along the Colorado River Trail to the junction at Red Mountain Trail, and take the road to the left, crossing the Colorado River and turning south to begin the climb up the eastern slopes of the Never Summer Mountains. The climb alternates between lush forests rich with wildflowers and open areas of rocky terrain. The sounds of songbirds serenade you, the dappled sunlight is entrancing, and the views of the Kawuneeche Valley to the south and the mountain ridges to the east are spectacular when seen through a fringe of aspens.

In the autumn, when the aspens turn a golden yellow, the vistas are even more dramatic. During summer, bright pink fireweed grows among gray rocks, producing a wildly contrasting color scheme. Once you top out, you can walk for miles along the service road for the Grand Ditch (see "Historic Attractions," in chapter 3), and the views in virtually all directions are compelling. Red Mountain in the southeast and Mount Cumulus to the west seem almost close enough to touch, and Howard and Lead mountains lie in the northwest. Watch the Colorado River snake southward through the Kawuneeche Valley. The trail begins at an elevation of 9,010 feet and climbs 1,200 feet.

**Lulu City Trail.** 3.7 miles one-way. Moderate. Access: Colorado River Trailhead on the west side of Trail Ridge Rd., 9.6 miles north of the Grand Lake Entrance Station.

This trail gains just 350 feet in elevation as it winds along the river flood plain, through lush vegetation, past an 1880s mine and several miners' cabins, and then along an old stage route into a subalpine forest, before arriving at the site of Lulu City. Founded in 1879 by prospectors hoping to strike gold and silver, it was abandoned within 10 years, and little remains of it today except the ruins of a few cabins. The beginning elevation is 9,010 feet.

✪ **Onahu Creek/Green Mountain Loop Trail.** 7-mile loop. Moderate to strenuous. Access: Onahu Creek Trailhead, 3.2 miles north of the Grand Lake Entrance Station.

From the trailhead there's about a mile's climb through forests of aspen, lodgepole pine, fir, and spruce to a bridge across Onahu Creek. Watch for wild berries as you hike—blueberries, strawberries, and occasionally huckleberries can be found here. A little over 2 miles from the trailhead, the path follows the creek a bit, where mossy rocks, boulders, and several bridges provide attractive areas for picnicking. The last bridge over Onahu Creek is just short of 3 miles from the trailhead, and once across, you'll approach the junction with Timber Creek Trail. Turn right (south), and you will climb somewhat steeply for about 0.5 miles before entering a forest of lodgepole pine so dense that it limits visibility. Shortly after the Tonahutu Trail joins from the east, you'll enter Big Meadows and hike along its western edge for about 0.5 miles. Big Meadows contains the remnants of Sam Stone's ranching efforts of the early 1900s, alongside wildflowers such as red elephant heads. From here, head west on Green Mountain Trail to Trail Ridge Road. It's only a short walk north from that point to get back to where you started. The initial elevation is 8,794 feet, and the elevation gain is 858 feet.

**Timber Lake Trail.** 4.8 miles one-way. Strenuous. Access: Timber Lake Trailhead on the east side of Trail Ridge Rd., 9.6 miles north of the Grand Lake Entrance Station.

The trail starts off fairly easy, crossing a meadow, open woodlands, and a bridge over Beaver Creek, but then begins climbing steeply. About 400 feet above the valley floor, it follows Timber Creek upstream. Then 3 miles from the trailhead, Long Meadows Trail joins the path, and a small tributary flows into the creek, providing abundant moisture to support numerous wildflowers, such as the delicate pink Parry's primrose and the lovely white marsh marigold. Climbing more steeply along short switchbacks will bring you to a meadow of

# Grand Lake Area Trails

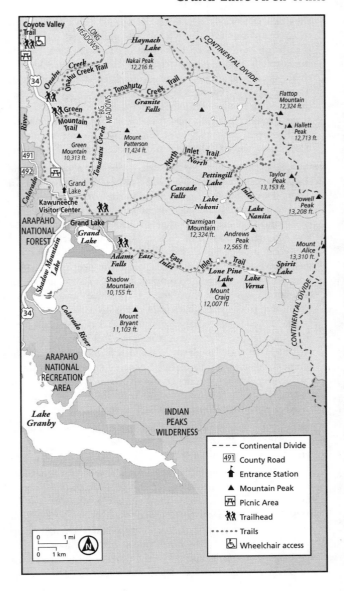

subalpine flowers. The striking roseroot, or king's crown with its cluster of small red-brown flowers, and the red and yellow paintbrush border the path as it follows Timber Creek. Winding through a subalpine forest, and then among rocks, the final switchback ascent brings you to the marshlike outlet of Timber Lake. A few trees accent the north shore of the lake, but the stark beauty of the spot is defined by rock, tundra, and snow even in midsummer. It's surrounded by the rugged northwestern flank of Mount Ida, whose summit is hidden. The hike begins at 9,000 feet and ascends another 2,060 feet.

## 3 Exploring the Backcountry

There are numerous opportunities in the park for backpacking and technical climbing, and hikers and climbers will generally find that the farther they go into the backcountry, the fewer humans they will meet. Some of the day hikes discussed above can also be done as overnight hikes. For example, the East Longs Peak Trail, which takes most people about 15 hours round-trip, is often completed over 2 days. Hikers can also combine various short trails to produce loops that can keep them in the park's backcountry for up to a week.

The Bear Lake area has several trails that can be combined for longer jaunts. The same is true in the Wild Basin area. The North Inlet and Tonahutu trails described below start at Grand Lake and lead to Flattop Mountain on the Continental Divide, where the trails connect to Bear Lake. Only your desire, your time constraints, and your ability will limit the number of trail combinations available to you.

✪ **North Inlet Trail.** 10.5 miles one-way. Strenuous. Access: Tonahutu/ North Inlet Trailhead off Colo. 278 out of Grand Lake.

The first 3.5 miles of this trail are described in the Cascade Falls Trail listing above. Past the falls, the trail continues following the North Inlet along a fairly gentle incline for about another 3 miles. Then you climb along several short switchbacks, eventually reaching the junction with Lake Nanita Trail (see below for description). For Flattop, take the left fork up the switchbacks along the north side of Hallett Creek, watching for—or at least listening to—the water as it cascades down the steep incline. The trail levels out a bit after the switchbacks, heading through a lovely subalpine forest and crossing Hallett Creek before ascending the steep walls on the western flank of Taylor, Otis, and Hallett peaks. The wildflower displays along the rest of the trail are some of the best in the park, particularly in July and August. As the path smoothes out again, tall rock cairns lead you over the tundra to the summit of Flattop. From here, you can turn right and hike down to Bear Lake (see "East-Side Day Hikes," above), turn left and take the Tonahutu Trail back to Grand Lake (see below), or turn around and follow this trail back. The beginning elevation is 8,540 feet, and there is an elevation gain of 3,784 feet.

The spur to Lakes Nokoni and Nanita heads south from the above trail about 7.5 miles from the trailhead. It crosses the North Inlet Gorge at North Inlet Falls and then leaves the waterway to head up the northeast side of Ptarmigan Mountain. Openings in the dense forest allow views into the North Inlet valley and Lake Solitude to the southeast. When you reach the bedrock at the tree line, it's not far to Lake Nokoni, which lies in a glacier-created basin 9.9 miles from the trailhead. Follow the trail another 1.1 miles through the subalpine forest to Lake Nanita, a much prettier lake than Nokoni, with Andrews Peak rising majestically on its far side. On calm days, the mountain's reflections in the lake are sublime. There is an elevation gain of 2,240 feet as you travel the 11 miles from the trailhead.

**Tonahutu Trail.** 12.8 miles one-way. Strenuous. Access: Tonahutu/North Inlet Trailhead off Colo. 278 out of Grand Lake.

Hike north on a gradual slope from the trailhead for just under a mile to where the 0.5-mile spur from the Kawuneeche Visitor Center joins the path. The incline steepens a bit, following Tonahutu Creek to the south end of Big Meadows, a rather marshy area. The trail keeps to the western edge of the meadows, where shade provides some respite from the sun, and continues northward. The Green Mountain Loop Trail (see "West-Side Day Hikes," above) junctions from the west about 3.6 miles from the trailhead. Continue past the log-cabin ruins and around the northern edge of Big Meadows. The trail follows the north bank of the Tonahutu Creek upstream, past Granite Falls (7.8 miles from the trailhead), crossing a stream flowing from Haynach Lakes (9.5 miles from the trailhead), and finally climbs up the west flank of the Continental Divide to Flattop Mountain. The initial elevation is 8,540 feet, and you'll gain another 3,784 feet. Parking at the Kawuneeche Visitor Center can shorten the trail by 0.4 miles and reduce the elevation gain to 3,604 feet. If you start this hike at the Green Mountain Trailhead, you'll shorten the trail to 11.1 miles, miss about half of Big Meadows, and reduce the elevation gain to 3,524 feet.

## BACKCOUNTRY CAMPING

The park has more than 100 small backcountry campsites, which may be reserved in advance. Permits are required and are available at the **Backcountry Office** in park headquarters and the **Kawuneeche Visitor Center** (see "Essentials," in chapter 3). Once at the park you can get a permit in person on the day you plan to set out. Reservations can be made ahead of time by mail (write to Backcountry Permits, Rocky Mountain National Park, Estes Park, CO 80517) anytime after March 1 for that calendar year. Phone reservations (☎ **970/586-1242,** or 970/586-1319 for the hearing impaired) are taken only between March 1 and May 15, and again after October 1 for that calendar year.

To obtain a permit, you'll have to supply the park service with your name, address with zip code, and telephone number; your planned itinerary with dates indicating where you plan to camp; and the number of persons in the party. You'll also need to pay an administration fee of $15, payable by cash or check, upon issue of the permit.

There are from one to nine campsites in each backcountry area, and each campsite can accommodate up to seven people. Rangers say that small parties have less impact on the wilderness, and generally experience more harmony on the trail. Parties of 8 to 12 people require special group sites especially set up to accommodate the greater impact.

In summer (June through September), backcountry use is highest, so camping is limited to 3 nights at any one site and 7 nights total. From October through May you may spend 14 nights total. An annual limit of 21 nights is also imposed. If you leave before you planned to, notify a ranger so your spot can be assigned to someone else.

Once you arrive at the park, check in with a ranger even if you already have the required permits. Rangers know the trails and camping areas well, and are happy to discuss possible destinations with hikers. They can give you the latest information about the trail you plan to take—whether there's still snow in

## Backcountry Equipment Checklist

Waterproof matches
Map and compass
Signal mirror
Water
Extra food
Pocket knife (Swiss Army's are terrific)
First-aid kit
Nylon cord
Sunglasses with ultraviolet protection
Wide-brimmed hat
UVA- and UVB-protection sunscreen and lip balm
Rain poncho and extra warm clothing
Flashlight with spare bulb and batteries
Toilet paper
Tent or tarp
Ground cloth
Sleeping bag (lightweight in summer)
Sleeping bag stuff sack (usable to hang food)
Sleeping pad (with repair kit if inflatable)
Small plastic or collapsible metal shovel
Maps and trail descriptions
Stove and fuel
Airtight food containers
Eating utensils
Lightweight cooking pot
Extra plastic freezer bags
Water-purifying pump (for wilderness trails)
Water-purifying tablets (in case of pump failure)
Extra gallon jug for water cache (depending on hike length)
Lightweight binoculars
Lightweight camera and film
Walking stick.

the area, recent animal sightings, and so forth. Also be certain to check on the weather forecast; the weather can change abruptly in the mountains, particularly on summer afternoons. Winds are constant visitors to the mountain peaks and can be deadly when combined with rain; so take clothing that can be layered, and don't forget storm gear. Although mosquitoes may not be as plentiful as they are in more humid climes, they do exist here, so carry insect repellent in your pack. The bulletin boards at trailheads will also provide good up-to-the-minute information about the trails.

When you reach your camping area, follow the signs indicating the campsite locations. Don't simply put up your tent anywhere, and don't dig a trench around your tent. Keep a tidy camp: Place garbage in sealed containers to pack it out, and hang your food from a tree at least 10 feet above the ground and 4 feet out from the trunk—this will keep it safe from bears and smaller animals. Scented items, including deodorant, should be kept out of your tent so they won't entice uninvited creatures inside. Many animals are attracted by the salt in sweat and urine, so place gear in a hanging bag and observe proper backcountry sanitation.

Backpackers should carry portable stoves since wood fires are permitted only at the few sites with metal fire rings. In addition to the designated backcountry campsites, there are about two dozen cross-country zones—in some of the least-accessible sections of the park—which are recommended only for those with excellent map and compass skills. Remember to leave an itinerary with someone at home in case of an emergency.

## 4  Biking & Mountain Biking

Bikes are not permitted off established roads at Rocky, and bicyclists will, in most cases, be sharing roadways with motor vehicles along narrow roads that have 5% to 7% gradients. However, bicyclists will still enjoy the challenge of the roadways and the beauty of the scenery. Remember, it's best to head out as early as possible because storms occur almost daily from June through September anytime after late morning. Storms cause dangerous lightning, wet and slippery road surfaces, and freezing temperatures that can lead to hypothermia.

One popular 16-mile ride with plenty of beautiful mountain views is the **Horseshoe Park/Estes Park Loop.** Head west from Estes Park on U.S. 34 past Aspenglen Campground and the park's Fall River entrance, and then turn back toward the east at the Deer Ridge Junction, following U.S. 36 through the Beaver Meadows park entrance. Allow 1 to 3 hours.

Bear Lake and Trail Ridge roads are also open to bicycles. Bear Lake Road climbs 1,500 feet over 8 miles from Moraine Park, a lovely glacier-created valley framed by mountains, to Bear Lake, the takeoff point for numerous trails into the backcountry. Stop at Sprague Lake and Glacier Gorge Junction along the way for parking, hiking, and photo opportunities. The round-trip takes about 2 to 4 hours.

Only strong cyclists should tackle Trail Ridge Road from the Grand Lake Entrance since it ascends 3,758 feet in just over 20 miles. About 10 miles of this attractive winding road are above 12,000 feet elevation—less oxygen and colder air. Start out as early as sunrise to avoid the heaviest traffic on the narrow road, and also to avoid an all-too-likely summer thunder (and lightning) storm above the tree line. Temporary shelter can be found at Milner Pass, Fall River Pass in the visitor center and store, and in an emergency, in comfort stations at Rock Cut and Rainbow Curve. Allow 4 to 6 hours round-trip.

Old Fall River Road is also open to bicycles, but mountain bikes are recommended for this rugged ride. See the sidebar "Old Fall River Road: A Step Back in Time," in chapter 3.

A free park brochure, available at visitor centers, provides a map and information on safety and regulations.

Tours, rentals, and repairs are available at **Colorado Bicycling Adventures,** 184 E. Elkhorn Ave., Estes Park (☎ **970/586-4241**). Rentals are $15 to $30 for a half day, and $21 to $50 for a full day, depending on the type of bike, with discounts for multiday rentals. You can also rent child carriers, car racks, and locks. The company offers road trips in the national park (downhill on paved roads) for $46 to $70, and off-road mountain bike tours outside the park for experienced riders for about $53 per person. Bike rentals are also available at similar rates from **Estes Park Mountain Shop,** 358 E. Elkhorn Ave. (☎ **800/504-6642** or 970/586-6548).

In Grand Lake, stop at **Rocky Mountain Sports,** 830 Grand Ave. (☎ **970/627-8124**), for repairs, maps, and rentals, at rates similar to those in Estes Park.

## 5   Climbing & Mountaineering

The south-facing cliffs of Lumpy Ridge, found along Black Canyon in the northeast corner of the park, are a favorite of rock climbers. To access the cliffs, head north out of Estes Park via MacGregor Avenue. Another area that's popular is the Diamond on Longs Peak, but it is a grueling 2-day vertical climb and should be attempted by only the most experienced rock climbers.

The rock walls that entice technical climbers are the same cliffs that birds of prey choose for nesting. Raptor populations have decreased radically since the 1960s, due to the increased use of pesticides, the loss of habitat, and hunting. Those drawn to the rough, craggy outcrops of Rocky Mountain National Park include peregrine and prairie falcons, Cooper's and red-tailed hawks, golden eagles, turkey vultures, and kestrels. They generally return to these mountains in March and April to choose nesting sites, and during this time—usually mid-March to mid-July—certain areas are closed to all humans. Check with the Backcountry Office or visitor centers to find out which locations are closed during your visit.

**CROSS-COUNTRY ZONES & TECHNICAL-CLIMBING BIVOUACS**   In addition to the designated backcountry campsites, there are about two dozen cross-country zones. With little traffic and no developed trails or campsites, cross-country zones are the most remote in the park. These isolated areas boast rough and rugged terrain, wet marshy areas, icy cold streams, and thick forests. In addition to the regulations for backcountry hiking and camping discussed above, these zones are limited to human foot traffic, persons expert in the use of map and compass and in "Leave No Trace" techniques. Fires are not permitted. Parties are limited to seven persons. Your camp must be at least 200 feet (70 steps) from any water source, must be out of sight and sound from any other party, and must be moved at least 1 mile each day; and your stay in any one zone is limited to 2 nights.

Technical climbers who expect to be out overnight usually set up a bivouac—a temporary, open-air encampment that is normally found at, or near the base of, a route or on the face of a climb. Designated bivouac zones have been established, and permits, available from the Backcountry Office (see above), are required for both the bivouac site and all vehicles parked at the trailhead. Tents are not permitted in bivouac zones. The site must be at least 3.5 miles from the trailhead; you may not sleep on vegetation, only on rock or snow. Climbers can't make camp until after sundown and must vacate before sunup. Climbing parties are limited to four persons, all of whom must climb.

Some areas restrict the total number of people allowed in bivouac zones, and reservations may be made for these locations after March 1 in person or by mail, and by phone until May 20 (see above for address and phone). The restricted areas as of this writing were Longs Peak, Black Lake, Notchtop Peak, and Skypond Area/Andrews Glacier. Other areas neither need nor accept reservations.

**GUIDES & GEAR**    The ✪ **Colorado Mountain School,** 351 Moraine Ave. (P.O. Box 1846), Estes Park, CO 80517 (☎ **888/CMS-7783** or 970/586-5758; www.cmschool.com; e-mail: cmschool@cmschool.com), is an AMGA accredited year-round guide service, and the sole concessionaire for technical climbing and instruction in Rocky Mountain National Park. The school has programs for all ages. The most popular climb is Longs Peak (the highest mountain in the park). It can be ascended by those without experience via the "Keyhole," but its north and east faces are for experts only. Rates vary, and the larger the group the less per person, but the base rate for one person for half- and full-day excursions ranges from $75 to $300. The school also offers lodging in a hostel-type setting (see the "Estes Park" section in chapter 6).

**Estes Park Mountain Shop,** 358 E. Elkhorn Ave. (☎ **800/504-6642** or 970/586-6548), has an indoor climbing gym and also offers climbing instruction and guided trips both in and near the national park, as well as a kids' outdoor adventure program in half- and full-day sessions and rentals and sales of climbing and camping equipment.

## 6 Educational Programs

The ✪ **Rocky Mountain Nature Association,** Rocky Mountain National Park, Estes Park, CO 80517 (☎ **800/816-7662** or 970/586-1258; www.rmna.org/bookstore; e-mail: seminars@ webaccess.net), offers a wide variety of seminars and workshops, ranging from a half day to several days in duration. The program began as a single course in the summer of 1962, and by 2000 the association offered well over 100 courses, including a number for children. Subjects vary but might include songbirds, flower identification, edible and medicinal herbs, painting, wildlife photography, tracking park animals, astronomy, human history, and edible mushrooms.

The nature association thinks of Rocky Mountain National Park as a "college on the crest of the continent," and uses it as an outdoor classroom. Field trips are a part of most seminars, and sometimes require more than average exertion.

Programs are scheduled from spring through fall, although most of them are held from June through August. Rates range from $25 to $75 for half- and full-day programs, and $85 to $195 for multiday programs. Nature Association members get 10% discounts. Participants are responsible for their own lodging and meals. Academic credit is available from Colorado State University for some of the longer courses, and all seminars qualify as teacher recertification units (one-half to three semester credits).

## 7   Fishing

You can fish four species of **trout** in the park streams and lakes: brown, rainbow, brook, and cutthroat, although the greenback cutthroat trout is limited to catch-and-release. Anglers 16 years and older must have a Colorado fishing license, and only artificial lures and flies are permitted. Children 12 and under may use worms or preserved fish eggs, though not in catch-and-release areas, where no bait whatsoever is allowed.

The only fish native to Rocky Mountain National Park are the greenback cutthroat and the Colorado River cutthroat. When the park area was first settled, fishing became quite popular, and people began stocking streams with non-native species. They even relocated trout to streams and lakes that had none. The National Park Service continued stocking non-native trout until 1968. That policy has been reversed, and since 1975, efforts have been made to remove non-native fish and to restore native species. Several waters with restored native fish are open for catch-and-release, using barbless hooks. These include Fern Lake and Fern Creek, Hidden Valley Beaver Ponds and Hidden Valley Creek (from August 1 to March 31), the North Fork of the Big Thompson River above

Lost Falls, Sandbeach Lake and Sandbeach Creek, Spruce Lake, and Timber Lake and Timber Creek.

Out of the 147 lakes in the park, only 50 are known to have fish populations. The cold water and the lack of a spawning habitat in high-altitude lakes prohibit fish reproduction. Of the lakes known to have fish, fishing is allowed at Sprague Lake just off Bear Lake Road; Lake Verna and Lone Pine Lake along the East Inlet Trail on the west side of the park; Lake of Glass, Loch Vale, and Mills Lake above Bear Lake; and Ypsilon Lake north of Fall River Road. Some of the park's lakes and streams are closed to fishing, including Bear Lake and Hunters Creek above Wild Basin Ranger Station.

A complete list of open and closed waters is available at visitor centers and ranger stations. The brochure also lists the possession limit, which is intentionally low to aid in restoration efforts. Anglers can also try out the fishing opportunities in the nearby national forests, and at the three lakes near the community of Grand Lake outside the park's west entrance (see chapter 6).

Among local outfitters offering fly-fishing instruction and guided trips are **Estes Angler** (☎ **800/586-2110** or 970/586-2110; www.estesangler.com) and **Scot's Sporting Goods,** 870 Moraine Ave. (☎ **970/586-2877**). Typical rates for a half-day guided fishing trip for two people is $175, and a 2-hour fly-fishing class for one costs about $25. Both outfitters also offer equipment rental.

## 8  Horseback Riding

Many of the national park's trails are open to horses and pack animals, including mules, ponies, llamas, and burros. There should be no more than 20 animals in a string, and their feed must be brought with you because grazing is not permitted. Generally, campgrounds and picnic areas are off-limits to riders; however, there are several designated "stock camps" in the backcountry (permit required). There are four sites posted for llama use only, and other sites are limited to 5 to 20 horses or other stock. Animals must be tied securely to the hitch rack provided at the site.

Cross-country travel is not permitted, and you must stay on maintained trails to prevent damage to vegetation. Horses do have the right-of-way, but it is your responsibility when overtaking hikers to make your presence known to them so that they have time to yield. Galloping is not allowed, and equestrians should slow to a walk when nearing or passing others.

Several outfitters provide guided rides, both in and outside the park. Typical prices are $20 for a 1-hour ride, $35 for 2 hours, $45 for 3 hours, $55 for a half day, and $80 for a full day. Highly recommended is the ✪ **Sombrero Ranch Stables's** breakfast ride, which runs from March through December and includes a 2-hour ride and an all-you-can-eat full breakfast for about $40. Sombrero has stables on the east side of the park opposite Lake Estes Dam, at 1895 Big Thompson Hwy. (U.S. 34) (☎ **970/586-4577;** www.sombrero.com). The company also offers horseback rides on the west side of the park in the Grand Lake area (☎ **970/627-3514**). Also in the Grand Lake area, **Winding River Resort** (☎ **970/627-3215**) offers 1- and 2-hour trail rides, plus kids' pony rides.

**Hi Country Stables** operates two stables inside the park that offer similar rides and rates: Glacier Creek Stables (☎ **970/586-3244**) and Moraine Park Stables (☎ **970/ 586-2327**). **National Park Village Stables,** at the Fall River Entrance of the national park on U.S. 34 (☎ **970/ 586-5269**), and the **Cowpoke Corner Corral,** at Glacier Lodge, 3 miles west of town, 2166 Colo. 66 (☎ **970/ 586-5890**), both offer similar rides and rates from May through September.

## 9  Winter Activities

Remember that winter in the high mountains comes earlier than in the low country, and it's generally much more severe. The center of Rocky Mountain National Park—Trail Ridge Road between Many Parks Curve on the east and the Colorado River Trailhead on the west—is closed to vehicular traffic from about mid-October to late May. Old Fall River Road is also closed, usually from September into early July. The exact dates of both closures depend on the weather. (See "When to Go," in chapter 2.)

Roads that remain open in the winter can be icy and snow-packed, so be sure you have snow tires or chains, and always check on road conditions at the visitor centers or entrance stations.

**HIKING**    There are several low-elevation trails on the east side of the park that are usually safe to hike in winter. The snow is generally too deep for hiking west of the Continental Divide. Of the trails described above, Cub Lake Trail, Gem Lake Trail, and the first part of the Fern Lake Trail, to The Pool, are all reasonably passable in winter. Two other relatively short trails are also recommended.

You can access the easy 3.5-mile **Upper Beaver Meadows Trail** from a closed gate on the west side of Upper Beaver Road, about 2 miles west of park headquarters. Inside the gate, a trail forks to the left and a road forks to the right. They connect at the other end of Beaver Meadows, so you can follow either of them. The trail crosses Beaver Brook and skirts the south side of the meadow, eventually bending north to meet the road in the parking area at the west end of the meadow. The road winds through the meadow north of the brook, and back to the starting point. Watch for elk near the water or at the edge of the trees. The initial elevation is 8,300 feet, with an elevation gain of 140 feet.

The other recommended trail for winter hikers is the moderate 2.5-mile **Chasm Falls Trail.** To get to the trailhead, turn west onto Endovalley Road off U.S. 34 at Horseshoe Park and drive to the road closure. From the parking lot, hike along Endovalley Road for about 1.5 miles to Old Fall River Road. Watch for ruins of the cabins where the prison laborers who built Old Fall River Road in the early 20th century lived. Head up Old Fall River Road (the right fork) about a mile to the falls. As you approach the falls, you'll notice lovely, but treacherous, ice formations—proceed very carefully. The beginning elevation is 8,960 feet, and there is a gain of 400 feet.

**ICE FISHING**    The same rules apply to ice fishing as to warm-weather fishing (see above). Check the ice carefully before venturing onto it.

**SKIING & SNOWSHOEING**    A growing number of people are discovering the joys of exploring Rocky Mountain National Park on cross-country skis and snowshoes. Snow conditions are often best from January through March. Snowshoeing has become especially popular in recent years. Made of lightweight materials with antislip surfaces, modern snowshoes have come a long way from those big, awkward "tennis rackets" some of us remember, and are a great way to explore the outdoors in winter. Snowshoes are conveniently available for rent at area sporting-goods stores. Among shops that rent snowshoes is **Colorado Bicycling Adventures,** 184 E. Elkhorn Ave., Estes Park (☎ 970/586-4241). Daily rental costs $10 per pair, including poles, and the company also offers 4-hour guided snowshoe tours into the park, including equipment, for $25 per person. See also "Supplies," under "FAST FACTS: Rocky Mountain National Park," in chapter 3.

If you're headed into the backcountry for cross-country skiing or snowshoeing, stop by park headquarters for maps, information on snow conditions, and a free backcountry permit if you plan to stay out overnight. Keep in mind that trails are not groomed. On winter weekends, rangers often lead guided snowshoe walks on the east side of the park and guided cross-country ski trips on the west side. Participants must supply their own equipment.

One popular winter recreation area for both skiing and snowshoeing is Bear Lake because of its numerous connecting trails. It's a good idea to be prepared to spend the night out if you are going any distance at all from the road. Check at visitor centers for current conditions, particularly avalanche danger areas. **Ice-skating** on Bear Lake is not prohibited, but the ice is not particularly good for skating—it's bumpy and usually covered with snow.

South of the park's east entrances, off Colo. 7 about 1 mile north of the community of Allenspark, is the ✪ **Wild Basin Trailhead.** Cross-country skiing along the trails in this area is becoming increasingly popular. A 2-mile road—the last mile is closed to motor vehicles in winter—winds through a subalpine forest to the Wild Basin Trailhead, where you can follow the 2.7-mile Ouzel Falls Trail (described above). Your chances for spotting birds, such as Clark's nutcrackers, Steller's jays, and the American dipper, along the trail are good. On winter weekends, the Colorado Mountain Club often opens a warming hut at the Wild Basin Ranger Station.

**SNOWMOBILING**    A recent National Park Service ruling has outlawed snowmobiling within the park, with one exception: On the park's west side, a snowmobile trail leads from the park into the adjacent **Arapaho National Forest.** This trail leaves U.S. 34 just north of the Kawuneeche Visitor Center and follows County Roads 491 and 492 west into the forest. Contact park visitor centers for current information.

# 5

# Camping in Rocky Mountain National Park

*F*or the best national-park experience, we believe you should not simply visit, look around, and leave, but rather you should move in and literally set up camp. The park becomes much more real when you see it during both nighttime and daytime. Gaze at its stars, fall asleep to the sound of a gentle breeze moving through the trees, and awaken to the songs of birds and the aroma of a nearby campfire. Because staying at a national park campground allows you to immerse yourself in the park experience, it is our first choice when vacationing here.

But the park campgrounds do fill up, and people have different needs and desires—some even want an occasional shower! Fortunately, just outside the national park, there are a number of commercial campgrounds with hot showers, RV hookups, and all the niceties, and there are also some very pleasant national-forest campgrounds. Whatever you want in a camping experience, you're likely to find it here. One note, though: Those with especially large RVs, such as 40-footers with slide-out rooms, will find only a limited number of national-park and national-forest sites that can easily accommodate their rigs, due to low-hanging trees, close boulders, and uneven ground. Owners of such vehicles are often happier camping at a nearby RV park.

## 1 Lodging & Dining Inside the Park

There are no lodging or full-service dining establishments inside the national park. See chapter 6 for lodgings and restaurants just outside the park entrances. The Fall River Store, at Fall River Pass on Trail Ridge Road, next to Alpine Visitor Center, has a snack bar and sells souvenirs and gifts. It is open summers only; check with visitor centers for current hours.

## 2  Camping Inside the Park

The park has almost 600 campsites scattered over five campgrounds, with nearly half of them at Moraine Park on the park's east side. Reservations are accepted at Moraine Park and Glacier Basin from Memorial Day to early September, and both are often completely booked in advance, especially on weekends, with the tent sites filling first. However, if by some odd quirk of fate a site is available, you won't be turned away.

As much as 5 months before your visit, contact the **National Park Reservation Service** (☎ 800/365-2267 or 301/722-1257; TDD 888/530-9796; http://reservations. nps.gov), or make reservations through the park's Web site (www.nps.gov/romo). Office hours are daily from 10am to 10pm Eastern Time, except Christmas and New Year's Day. Payment can be made by credit card (Discover, MasterCard, Visa) or by check or money order (allow at least 21 days), which must be received within 7 days of making your reservation. Payment cannot be made at the park for these reservations. You will receive a reservation number to identify you when you arrive at the park. If your plans change, call **NPRS Customer Account Services** (☎ 800/388-2733). Cancellations are subject to a fee, depending upon when the cancellation is received.

For other camping information, call the park (☎ 970/586-1206). In summer, arrive early if you hope to snare one of the first-come, first-served campsites.

✪ **Moraine Park Campground,** our favorite because we have always seen elk and other wildlife there, has 247 sites and is located on the west side of Bear Lake Road not far from the Moraine Park Museum. **Glacier Basin Campground,** which is about 500 feet higher in elevation than Moraine Park, is farther down Bear Lake Road on its east side and has 150 sites. Both campgrounds have tent sites—some are set well back from the road—and sites for pickup campers and larger rigs. Glacier Basin also offers a group camping area (small, medium, and large sites from $35 to $65). **Aspenglen Campground** is just inside the Fall River entrance to the park and has 54 tent and RV campsites. The other campground on the east side of the park is ✪ **Longs Peak,** located off Colo. 7 south of Estes Park, with 26 sites for tents only. **Timber Creek**

**Campground** is about 7 miles north of the Grand Lake entrance and has 100 sites for tents and RVs.

There are rest rooms accessible for travelers with disabilities at all campgrounds except Longs Peak and Aspenglen, and there is an accessible backcountry campsite at Sprague Lake, open in summer only. The amphitheaters are fully accessible at Moraine Park and Aspenglen, moderately accessible at Glacier Basin, and only marginally accessible at Timber Creek. Three campgrounds are open year-round—Timber Creek, Moraine Park, and Longs Peak—but no water is available at the campgrounds from October to late May. Aspenglen and Glacier Basin are closed from November through April.

Camping fees are additional to park entrance fees; they are $16 per night when water is available (generally during the summer), and $10 in the off-season, when water is turned off. No showers or RV hookups are available in the park, although drinking water is available in summer. Quiet hours are in force between 10pm and 6am; pets are allowed but must be in your tent or vehicle, or on a leash, and they should never be left alone. Summer camping is limited to 7 days, except at Longs Peak, where the limit is 3 days; the winter camping limit is 14 days.

## 3  Camping Near the Park on the East Side

There are several full-service commercial campgrounds in Estes Park, where you will find clean, well-maintained bathhouses, and fairly level RV sites, but fewer trees and less space between sites than in most national-park and national-forest campgrounds. Pets are generally accepted at commercial campgrounds, although owners must keep pets on leashes and clean up after them. Below is a list of privately owned campgrounds, and national-forest campgrounds, which are similar to national-park campgrounds, although their regulations are usually a bit less restrictive.

**Blue Arrow R.V. Park & Campground.** 1665 Colo. 66 (P.O. Box 1566), Estes Park, CO 80517. ☎ **800/582-5342** or 970/586-5342. www.estespark. com/bluearrow. E-mail: mgr-ba@cwscommunities.com. 168 sites. Rates for 2 $20–$29. MC, V. Open Apr to mid-Oct.

Located close to the national park's Beaver Meadows entrance, this campground boasts 30 open and wooded acres with grand views in all directions. There are several historic buildings on the property, plus a convenience store, laundry facilities, playgrounds, a dump station, sites to accommodate people with disabilities, and a recreation room.

**Estes Park Campground.** Colo. 66 (P.O. Box 3517), Estes Park, CO 80517. ☎ **888/815-2029** (reservations) or 970/586-4188. www.estes-park.com/epcampground. E-mail: epcampground@estes-park.com. 68 sites. Rates for 2 $19–$21 with no hookups, $22–$24 with hookups. AE, DISC, MC, V. Open late May to mid-Sept.

Located at the end of the road, 1 mile past the YMCA of the Rockies, and with the national park on two sides, this attractive campground offers glorious views and lots of quiet. Most campsites are nestled among pine trees and are perfect for tenters and pickup campers; only 15 have water and electric hookups. There are modern rest rooms with showers, a playground, a dump station, and firewood and ice available to purchase.

**Estes Park KOA.** 2051 Big Thompson Ave., Estes Park, CO 80517. ☎ **800/KOA-1887** (reservations) or 970/586-2888. www.koakampgrounds.com. E-mail: estesparkkoa@compuserve.com. 84 sites. Rates for 2 $22 with no hookups, $28–$30 with hookups (including cable TV); $44–$52 Kamping Kabin. DISC, MC, V. Open late Apr to mid-Oct.

Scenically located 1 mile east of Estes Park on U.S. 34, across from Lake Estes and within walking distance of the Big Thompson River, this KOA has a snack bar, convenience store, laundry, LP gas, a playground, and a miniature-golf course, but unlike most KOAs, it has no swimming pool.

**Mary's Lake Campground.** 2120 Mary's Lake Rd. (P.O. Box 2514), Estes Park, CO 80517. ☎ **800/445-6279** or 970/586-4411. Fax 970/586-4493. www.gocampingamerica.com/maryslake. E-mail: maryslake@aol.com. 150 sites. Rates for 2 $21 with no hookups, $26–$28 with hookups. Rates include cable TV. AE, DISC, MC, V. Open May–Sept.

This campground has beautiful mountain views and campsites for everything from tents to 40-foot RVs, with full hookups. Facilities include bathhouses, laundry, dump station, playground, basketball court, small store, heated swimming pool, and game room. Fishing licenses, bait, and tackle, for shore fishing at the lake and stream fishing in the national park, are available.

**National Park Resort, Cabins, and Camping.** 3501 Fall River Rd., Estes Park, CO 80517. ☎ **970/586-4563.** www.natlparkresort.com. E-mail: natlparkresort@aol.com. 92 sites, 9 lodging units. Rates for 2 $23–$25 with no hookups, $27–$30 with hookups. Cabins $90–$150 double. DISC, MC, V. Campground open May–Sept; motel units open spring–fall; cabins open year-round.

This wooded campground can accommodate both tents and RVs. Full hookups include electric, water, sewer, and cable TV. Facilities include bathhouses, a grocery store, and a livery stable. There are also four cabins with bathrooms (showers only), fireplaces, and fully equipped kitchens; and five motel units with shower/tub or shower-only bathrooms. Two of the motel units have kitchenettes and the other three have small refrigerators and microwaves. A coin-operated laundry is nearby.

✪ **Spruce Lake R.V. Park.** 1050 Mary's Lake Rd., Estes Park, CO 80517. ☎ **970/586-2889.** 110 sites. Rates for 2 $33–$35 with hookups. $2 fee for cable TV. Discounted rates at beginning and end of season. DISC, MC, V. Open Apr 1–Oct 15.

This meticulously maintained campground offers a heated pool, free miniature golf, a large playground, a stocked private fishing lake, large sites, and spotless bathhouses. There are Sunday pancake breakfasts, weekly ice-cream socials, bingo, and fishing tournaments. Ground tents are not permitted. Reservations are strongly recommended, especially in summer.

**ROOSEVELT NATIONAL FOREST**   There are two established forest service campgrounds within easy driving distance of the park's east entrances: ✪ **Olive Ridge,** 14.5 miles south of Estes Park along Colo. 7, not far from Allenspark, has pleasant, shady, well-spaced sites and an amphitheater. A less-developed campground, for those who carry their own drinking water, is **Meeker Park Overflow,** about 12 miles south of Estes Park on Colo. 7. Both campgrounds have picnic tables, fire rings, and vault toilets and can accommodate some RVs, but neither has hookups.

In addition, dispersed camping—in undeveloped areas—is allowed in some parts of the forest, but check with forest service offices before setting up camp. In Estes Park, a **Forest Service Information Center** is located at 161 Second St. (☎ **970/586-3440**); it's open daily in summer and has limited hours for several days a week in winter, depending on staff and volunteer availability. For year-round information, contact the **Forest Service Information Center,** 1311 S. College Ave., Fort Collins, CO 80524 (☎ **970/498-2770**); or the **Rocky Mountain Region office,** P.O. Box 25127, Lakewood,

CO 80225 (☎ **303/236-9431;** www.fs.fed.us/r2). Forest information is also available at the national park's Lily Lake Visitor Center (see "Visitor Centers & Information," in chapter 3).

For reservations (Olive Ridge Campground only), contact the **National Recreation Reservation Service** (☎ **877/ 444-6777;** TDD 877/833-6777l; www.reserveusa.com). Reservations can be made from 5 days to 8 months in advance, and there is a nonrefundable $8.65 reservation fee in addition to campground fees.

## 4 Camping Near the Park on the West Side

✪ **Elk Creek Campground and RV Park.** Golf Course Rd., County Rd. 48 (Box 549), Grand Lake, CO 80447. ☎ **800/355-2733** or 970/627-8502. www.coloradodirectory.com/elkcreekcamp. E-mail: elkcreek@rkymtnhi.com. 70 sites. Rates for 2 $18–$20 with no hookups, $20–$24 with hookups; $39 Camper Cabins. AE, DISC, MC, V. From Grand Lake head north on U.S. 34 about 0.25 miles and turn left onto Golf Course Rd. for 0.25 miles. Open May–Oct.

Just outside the national park, this well-maintained commercial campground has tent and RV sites in an attractive wooded setting. A championship golf course is just 0.25 miles away, and horseback riding is available nearby. Firewood is sold at the office for use in the campsite fire rings. On the grounds there are a stocked pond with license-free trout fishing, a playground, recreation and game rooms, horseshoes, volleyball, a convenience store, a laundry, and a dump station. Propane can be purchased daily from 9am to 5pm. Hot showers are available year-round, and snowmobile and cross-country ski trails are nearby. Reservations are strongly recommended from Memorial Day to Labor Day.

**Winding River Resort.** County Rd. 491 (Box 629), Grand Lake, CO 80447. ☎ **800/282-5121** (reservations) or 970/627-3215. Fax 970/627-5003. www.windingriverresort.com. E-mail: trailboss@rkymtnhi.com. 150 sites. Rates for 2 $20 with no hookups, $22–$24 with hookups, $35 Camper Cabins, $70–$130 double full cabins and lodge units. AE, DISC, MC, V. From Grand Lake, head north on U.S. 34 about 1.5 miles and turn left onto County Rd. 491 (across from the Kawuneeche Visitor Center) for 1.5 miles. Open mid-May through Sept.

Adjacent to Rocky Mountain National Park, Winding River is a good choice for campers seeking the forest experience of a national-parklike campground, but with hot showers, full

## Campgrounds

| Campground | Elev. | Total Sites | RV Hookups | Dump Station | Toilets | Drinking Water | Showers | Fire Pits/ Grills | Laundry | Public Phones | Reserve | Fees | Open |
|---|---|---|---|---|---|---|---|---|---|---|---|---|---|
| | | | | | | In the Park | | | | | | | |
| Aspenglen | 8,230 | 54 | 0 | no | yes | yes | no | yes | no | no | no | $16 | May–Oct |
| Glacier Basin | 8,600 | 150 | 0 | yes | yes | yes | no | yes | no | yes | yes | $16 | May–Oct |
| Longs Peak | 9,400 | 26 | 0 | no | yes | yes | no | yes | no | no | no | $10/$16* | Year-round |
| Moraine Park | 8,150 | 247 | 0 | yes | yes | yes | no | yes | no | yes | yes | $10/$16* | Year-round |
| Timber Creek | 8,900 | 100 | 0 | yes | yes | yes | no | yes | no | yes | no | $10/$16* | Year-round |
| | | | | | | Near Park's East Side | | | | | | | |
| Blue Arrow RV Park | 8,100 | 168 | 168 | yes | yes | yes | yes | yes | yes | yes | yes | $20–$29 | Apr to mid-Oct |
| Estes Park Campground | 8,200 | 68 | 15 | yes | yes | yes | yes | yes | yes | no | yes | $19–$24 | late May to mid-Sept |
| Estes Park KOA | 7,500 | 84 | 62 | yes | yes | yes | yes | no | yes | yes | yes | $22–$30 | Apr 25–Oct 19 |
| Mary's Lake | 8,200 | 150 | 90 | yes | yes | yes | yes | yes | yes | yes | yes | $21–$28 | May–Sept |
| Meeker Park | 8,600 | 29 | 0 | no | yes | no | no | yes | no | no | no | $6 | Mem Day–Lab Day |
| National Park Resort | 8,200 | 92 | 88 | yes | yes | yes | yes | yes | no | yes | yes | $23–$30 | May–Sept |
| Olive Ridge | 8,350 | 55 | 0 | no | yes | yes | no | yes | no | no | yes | $12 | mid-May to Oct |
| Spruce Lake RV Park | 7,622 | 110 | 110 | yes | yes | yes | yes | yes | yes | yes | yes | $33–$35 | Apr 1–Oct 15 |
| | | | | | | Near Park's West Side | | | | | | | |
| Arapaho Bay | 8,320 | 84 | 0 | no | yes | yes | yes | yes | no | no | yes | $12 | Mem Day–Lab Day |
| Elk Creek | 8,400 | 70 | 33 | yes | yes | yes | yes | yes | yes | yes | yes | $18–$24 | May–Oct |
| Green Ridge | 8,500 | 77 | 0 | yes | yes | yes | no | yes | no | no | yes | $12 | May–Oct |
| Stillwater | 8,350 | 129 | 20 | yes | yes | yes | yes | yes | no | yes | yes | $12–$20 | Year-round |
| Sunset Point | 8,350 | 25 | 0 | no | yes | yes | no | yes | no | no | no | $15 | Mem Day–Lab Day |
| Willow Creek | 8,130 | 35 | 0 | no | yes | yes | no | yes | no | no | no | $10 | May–Oct |
| Winding River | 8,672 | 150 | 98 | yes | yes | yes | yes | yes | yes | yes | yes | $20–$24 | mid-May to Sept |

*These fees are winter (when the water is turned off)/summer

RV hookups, and all the other amenities of a commercial campground. In addition, Winding River offers an abundance of activities, ranging from horseshoes to horseback riding ($20 for a 1-hour trail ride, $35 for a 2-hour ride), plus hayrides, ice-cream socials, and chuck wagon breakfasts. There's also a petting zoo, playground, convenience store, and a self-serve laundry. In addition to campsites, there are a variety of cabins and lodge units.

**ARAPAHO NATIONAL FOREST & NATIONAL RECREATION AREA**   The forest service campgrounds that are close to the park's west entrance are located around the lakes in the area. All five campgrounds have boat ramps. The most developed is **Stillwater Campground,** located off U.S. 34 on the west bank of Lake Granby, about 7 miles south of the west park entrance. Stillwater has showers, and water and electric hookups at 35 sites (summer only); a limited number of sites are open in winter, although there is no water available. **Green Ridge Campground,** about 5 miles south of the national park on U.S. 34 and then 1 mile south on County Road 66, offers modern rest rooms, picnic tables, and fire grates. **Willow Creek Campground** is located on Willow Creek Reservoir (about 10 miles south of the park on U.S. 34 and then about 4 miles west on County Road 40), and has picnic tables and vault toilets. **Arapaho Bay Campground** is at the eastern tip of Lake Granby and is reached by an all-weather gravel road that follows the lake's south shore. It has drinking water, vault toilets, and access to hiking trails into the Indian Peaks Wilderness Area. **Sunset Point Campground,** on the south shore of Lake Granby about a mile east of U.S. 34, offers tree-shaded sites, picnic tables, and vault toilets. The above five U.S. Forest Service campgrounds are within the Arapaho National Recreation Area, and in addition to camping fees, campers must pay the recreation-area entrance fee of $5 per vehicle for 1 day, $10 for 3 days, or $15 for 7 days.

Dispersed camping is also allowed in some areas of the forest; check with forest service offices for locations and regulations. For information on both the forest and the recreation area, contact the **Sulphur Ranger District office,** P.O. Box 10, Granby, CO 80446 (☎ **970/887-4100**). The U.S. Forest

Service's **Rocky Mountain Region office,** P.O. Box 25127, Lakewood, CO 80225 (☎ **303/236-9431;** www.fs.fed.us/r2), can also provide information.

For campsite reservations (Arapaho Bay, Green Ridge, and Stillwater only), contact the **National Recreation Reservation Service** (☎ **877/444-6777;** TDD 877/833-6777; www.reserveusa.com). Reservations can be made from 5 days to 8 months in advance; there is a nonrefundable $8.65 reservation fee in addition to camping fees.

## 5  Camper Services & Supplies

The only retail store inside the park other than visitor center/museum bookstores is the Fall River Store, next to Alpine Visitor Center at Fall River Pass on Trail Ridge Road. Open only in summer, it sells a wide variety of souvenirs, gift items, and outdoor clothing, and has a snack bar. There are no other stores, laundries, or showers in the park, but all can be found just outside the main park entrances.

For supplies in Estes Park, head for **Country Supermarket,** 0.75 miles from the Beaver Meadows entrance, or **Rocky Mountain Gateway,** adjacent to the Fall River Visitor Center, which also has a coin-operated laundry. In Grand Lake, stop at the **Mountain Food Market** or the **Circle D** for groceries and picnic supplies. Camping and outdoor-sports supplies and equipment are available in Estes Park at **Outdoor World, Rocky Mountain Connection,** and **Estes Park Mountain Shop.** See "Supplies," under "Fast Facts: Rocky Mountain National Park," in chapter 3, for exact addresses and other details.

**Dad's Maytag Laundry** offers a variety of laundering options in Estes Park, and in Grand Lake stop at **Mountain Village Laundromat.** See "Laundries," under "Fast Facts: Rocky Mountain National Park," in chapter 3.

For public showers in Estes Park, head for **Dad's Maytag Laundry** (☎ **970/586-2025**) in Stanley Village, a shopping center at the intersection of U.S. Highways 34 and 36 across from the town visitor center. Showers cost $3 for adults and $2.50 for children 12 and under, and towels can be rented for 50¢. Shampoo, razors, and soap are available for purchase. From Memorial Day to mid-August, it's open daily from 7am to 9:30pm; hours the rest the year are from 7:30am to 7:30pm daily. In Grand Lake, public showers are available at **Elk Creek Campground and RV Park** (see above), daily from 8am to 1pm and 2 to 8pm, at a cost of $4 per person; and **Winding River Resort** (see above) during similar hours for $5 per person.

Although there are no towing or repair facilities inside the park, **Bob's Amoco** in Estes Park, and **DJ Towing** in Granby, on the west side of the park, both offer 24-hour towing and road service and can handle large vehicles. See "Car Trouble/Towing Services," under "Fast Facts: Rocky Mountain National Park," in chapter 3.

# 6

# Gateway Towns & the National Forests

*R*ocky Mountain National Park straddles the Continental Divide between Estes Park on the east and Grand Lake on the west. These two towns guard the entrances to the park, and we recommend making either of them your home base for a visit to the park. If you prefer, it is certainly possible to base yourself in Fort Collins, Loveland, or Boulder on the east, and Granby or Winter Park on the west. Denver is another possibility, and you can head to either side of the park from there; but staying there means you won't have much time to do any real exploring.

Don't forget that Rocky Mountain National Park isn't the only outdoor experience in town. Nature's beauty does not suddenly stop at the park's boundaries, and there are plenty of things to see and do just outside the park—and within an easy and scenic drive of an hour or two. The Arapaho and Roosevelt national forests adjacent to the park offer some of the best fishing and outdoor recreational opportunities in the area, and an outing to either of them will greatly enhance your vacation experience.

## 1 Estes Park

71 miles NW of Denver, 30 miles W of Loveland, 42 miles SW of Fort Collins, 34 miles NW of Boulder

Unlike most Colorado mountain communities, which got their starts in mining, Estes Park (elevation 7,522 ft.) has always been a resort town. Long known by Utes and Arapahos, it was "discovered" in 1859 by rancher Joel Estes. He soon sold his homestead to Griff Evans, who built it into a dude ranch. One of Evans's guests, the Welsh Earl of Dunraven, was so taken with the region that he purchased most of the valley and operated it as a private game reserve, until thwarted by other settlers such as W. E. James, who built Elkhorn Lodge as a "fish ranch" to supply Denver restaurants.

But the growth of Estes Park is inextricably linked to two individuals: Freelan Stanley and Enos Mills. Stanley, a Bostonian who, with his brother Francis, invented the kerosene-powered Stanley Steamer automobile in 1899, settled in Estes Park in 1907. The brothers launched a Stanley Steamer shuttle service from Denver, and in 1909 built the landmark Stanley Hotel. Mills, an innkeeper-turned-conservationist, was one of the prime advocates for the establishment of Rocky Mountain National Park. Although not as well known as John Muir, Mills is an equally important figure in the history of the U.S. conservation movement. His tireless efforts as an author and stump speaker increased sentiment nationwide for preserving our wild lands, and resulted in the bill that set aside 400 square miles for Rocky Mountain National Park in 1915.

The larger of Rocky's two gateway towns, Estes Park offers a wide variety of shops, several interesting museums describing some of the human history of the area, and excellent lodging and dining.

## ESSENTIALS

**VISITOR INFORMATION  The Estes Park Chamber Resort Association** (☎ **800/443-7837** or 970/586-4431; fax 970/586-6336; www.estesparkresort.com) runs a tourist information center on U.S. 34 just east of its junction with U.S. 36 and with access from both highways. The association can also help you find suitable accommodations (see "Where to Stay," below).

**PICNICKING/CAMPING SUPPLIES**  Just three-quarters of a mile from the Beaver Meadows entrance to the park is **Country Supermarket,** with a wide range of supplies and groceries, and outside the Fall River entrance the **Village Grocery** sells groceries and supplies in summer only. See "Fast Facts," in chapter 3, and "Camper Services & Supplies," in chapter 5.

**CALENDAR OF EVENTS**  Artwalk and Jazz Festival, mid-May; the Wool Market, mid-June; the Scandinavian Mid-Summer Festival, on the weekend closest to the summer solstice; the Rooftop Rodeo and Western Heritage Days, third week in July; Scottish-Irish Highland Festival, the weekend after Labor Day in September; and Autumn Gold—A Festival of Brats and Bands, the last weekend in September.

**OUTDOOR PURSUITS**   There are numerous opportunities for camping, hiking, mountain biking, fishing, and winter activities on the national-forest lands surrounding the national park. See "Roosevelt National Forest" and "Arapaho National Forest & National Recreation Area," below, for more details. For the addresses of U.S. Forest Service offices, see "Getting Started: Information & Reservations," in chapter 2.

For information on stores that sell and rent outdoor and camping equipment, see "Camper Services & Supplies," in chapter 5.

## WHAT TO SEE & DO

✪ **Enos Mills Homestead Cabin.** 6760 Colo. 7 (opposite Longs Peak Inn). ☎ **970/586-4706.** Free admission (but donations welcome). Memorial Day to Labor Day, usually Tues–Sun 11am–4pm, but call to confirm. By appointment in other seasons.

This 1885 cabin and homestead belonged to the late–19th- and early–20th-century conservationist, Enos Mills, an enthusiastic advocate for the outdoors in general and the Rocky Mountains in particular, and a major force behind the establishment of Rocky Mountain National Park. A short walk down a nature trail brings you to the cabin, where members of the Mills family discuss his life and work. Memorabilia in the cabin include copies of the 15 books written by Mills and the cameras he used to take thousands of photos of the mountains he loved. Summer nature walks (call for current schedule and rates) are available by appointment, and evening talks are scheduled during the winter. Also on the premises are a bookshop, photo gallery, and nature center.

**Estes Park Aerial Tramway.** 420 E. Riverside Dr. ☎ **970/586-3675.** Admission $8 adults, $4 children 6–11, free for children 5 and under. Summer daily 9am–6:30pm.

This tram provides panoramic views of Longs Peak and the Continental Divide, plus Estes Park village itself. Its lower terminal is a block south of the post office. You'll find a gift shop, snack bar, and observation deck with binoculars (25¢) at the upper terminal on the summit of Prospect Mountain, and numerous trails converge atop the mountain.

# Estes Park

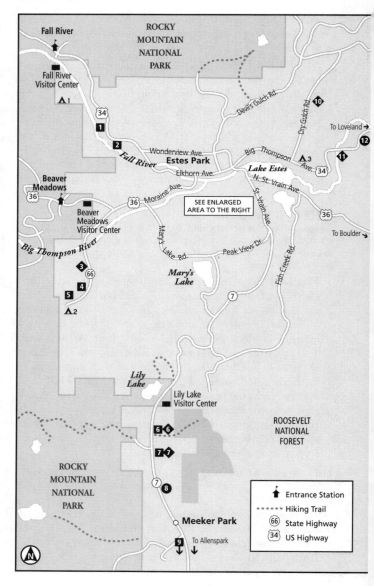

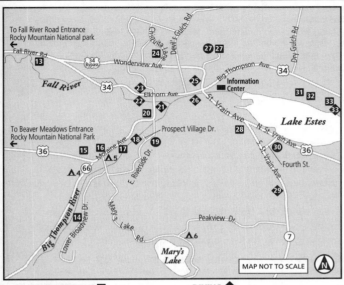

**ACCOMMODATIONS** ■
All Budget Inn **15**
Allenspark Lodge Bed & Breakfast **9**
Alpine Trail Ridge Inn **16**
Aspen Lodge at Estes Park **7**
Baldpate Inn **6**
Best Western Lake Estes Resort **32**
Big Thompson Timberlane Lodge **17**
Boulder Brook **2**
Colorado Mountain School **20**
Comfort Inn **31**
The Eagle Manor **24**
Estes Park Center/YMCA of the Rockies **5**
Fawn Valley Inn **1**
Glacier Lodge **4**
Holiday Inn **28**
Lake Shore Lodge **33**
Romantic RiverSong Inn **14**
Stanley Hotel **27**
Streamside Cabins **13**

**CAMPGROUNDS** ▲
Blue Arrow RV Park & Campground ▲4
Estes Park Campground ▲2
Estes Park KOA ▲3
Mary's Lake Campground ▲6
National Park Resort, Cabins, and Camping ▲1
Spruce Lake R.V. Park ▲5

**DINING** ◆
Andrea's of Estes **23**
Aspen Lodge Dining Room **7**
Baldpate Inn **6**
Bob & Tony's Pizza **22**
The Dunraven Inn **3**
Ed's Cantina & Grill **26**
The Egg & I **25**
Estes Park Brewery **19**
Grumpy Gringo **11**
Lazy B Ranch **10**
Molly B's **21**
Silverado at Lake Shore Lodge **33**
Timberline Family Restaurant **29**

**ATTRACTIONS** ●
Enos Mills Homestead Cabin **8**
Estes Park Aerial Tramway **19**
Estes Park Area Historical
  Museum **30**
Michael Ricker Pewter Casting
  Studio and Museum **12**
Stanley Museum of Colorado **27**

**Estes Park Area Historical Museum.** 200 Fourth St. at U.S. 36. ☎ **970/586-6256** or 970/586-6029. www.estes.on-line.com\epmuseum. E-mail: epmuseum@juno.com. Admission $2.50 adults, $2 seniors 60 and older, $1 children 12 and under, $10 maximum for families. May–Oct Mon–Sat 10am–5pm, Sun 1–5pm; Nov–Apr Fri–Sat 10am–5pm, Sun 1–5pm; extended Dec holiday hours.

The lives of early homesteaders in Estes Park are depicted in this excellent small museum, which includes a completely furnished turn-of-the-century log cabin, an original Stanley Steamer Car, and a changing exhibit gallery. The museum also features a permanent "Tracks in Time" exhibit that helps visitors see the impact that ordinary people, from the region's Native Americans and women pioneers to today's area residents and travelers, have had on Estes Park. You can also see Rocky Mountain National Park's original headquarters building, which has been moved here. In addition, the museum sponsors a variety of programs and distributes a historical-walking-tour brochure on downtown Estes Park.

**Michael Ricker Pewter Casting Studio & Museum.** 2050 Big Thompson Ave. ☎ **800/373-9837** or 970/586-2030. www.ricker.com. Free admission. Summer Mon–Thurs 9am–9pm, Fri–Sat 9am–8pm, Sun 10am–6pm; winter Mon–Sat 9am–5pm, Sun 11am–5pm.

Ricker is an internationally recognized artist and sculptor, whose works have been displayed in the Great Hall of Commerce in Washington, D.C., and at both Disneyland and Disney World. This museum and gallery has more than 1,000 pewter sculptures, including Ricker's masterpiece, Park City, claimed to be the world's largest miniature pewter sculpture. Free guided tours are available daily.

**Stanley Museum of Colorado.** Downstairs lobby of the Stanley Hotel, 333 Wonderview Ave. ☎ **970/577-1903.** Free admission. Daily 10am–4pm.

At this branch of the Stanley Museum of Kingfield, Maine, you can see exhibits on the life and work of F. O. Stanley and his family. Stanley, with his brother Francis, invented the Stanley Steam Car (more popularly known as the Stanley Steamer) in 1899, and in 1907 brought a fleet of his cars to Estes Park, built the Stanley Hotel, and began a shuttle service from Denver to bring tourists to the area.

## WHERE TO STAY

For help in finding accommodations in and around Estes Park, call the **Estes Park Chamber Resort Association Lodging**

**Referral Service** (☎ **800/44-ESTES** or 970/586-4431; www.estesparkresort.com). National chains represented here include **Best Western Lake Estes Resort,** 1650 Big Thompson Ave. (U.S. 34), Estes Park, CO 80517 (☎ **800/292-8439** or 970/586-3386), with rates of $120 to $130 double from mid-June to mid-September, and $50 to $85 double the rest of the year; **Comfort Inn,** 1450 Big Thompson Ave. (☎ **800/ 228-5150** or 970/586-2358), charging $85 to $190 double in summer, and $55 to $135 double the rest of the year; and **Holiday Inn,** U.S. 36 and Colo. 7 (P.O. Box 1468), Estes Park, CO 80517 (☎ **800/803-7837** or 970/586-2332), charging $129 to $139 double in summer, and $75 to $119 double the rest of the year. See also the listings "National Park Resort, Cabins, and Camping," and "Winding River Resort," in chapter 5.

Although many lodging facilities in the Estes Park area do not have air-conditioning, it is seldom needed at this elevation. Unless otherwise noted, pets are not permitted. Taxes add about 8% to hotel bills. Highest rates here, sometimes dramatically higher, are in summer.

**All Budget Inn.** 945 Moraine Ave., Estes Park, CO 80517. ☎ **800/ 628-3438** or 970/586-3485. www.estes-park.com/allbudget. 15 units. TV TEL. Summer $69–$99, rest of year $49–$69. MC, V. Pets accepted.

This pleasant motel offers simple rooms with homey touches such as fresh flowers, and nature prints adorn the white walls. Units have firm queen beds, a coffee pot and coffee, small refrigerator, and shower-tub combos; some units have kitchenettes and private balconies.

**Allenspark Lodge Bed & Breakfast.** Colo. 7 Business Loop (P.O. Box 247), Allenspark, CO 80510. ☎ **303/747-2552.** 14 units, 7 with bathroom. $65–$135 double. Rates include breakfast. AE, DISC, MC, V. Children 14 and over welcome.

There's a historic ambience to this three-story lodge, built in 1933 of native stone and hand-hewn ponderosa-pine logs. The lodge is located 16 miles south of Estes Park in a tiny village at the southeast corner of the national park, and all rooms offer mountain views and original handmade 1930s pine furniture. Guests share the Great Room and its stone fireplace; Ping-Pong and videos in the recreation room; and books in the library. Complimentary afternoon and evening coffee, tea, and cookies are served. There are also a hot tub, self-service laundry, conference rooms, an espresso coffee shop, and a wine-and-beer bar.

✪ **Alpine Trail Ridge Inn.** 927 Moraine Ave., Estes Park, CO 80517. ☎ **800/ 233-5023** or 970/586-4585. Fax 970/586-6249. www.alpinetrailridgeinn. com. E-mail: alpine@alpinetrailridgeinn.com. 48 units. TV TEL. First 3 weeks of May and mid-Sept to mid-Oct $52–$81 double; late May to mid-June and mid-Aug to mid-Sept $64–$92; mid-June to mid-Aug plus holidays and special events $81–$108 double. AE, CB, DC, DISC, MC, V. Closed mid-Oct through Apr.

The Alpine offers a variety of accommodations to suit every need. Seven units have showers only, the rest have tub-shower combos, and each has a refrigerator, a table, and upholstered chairs. Largest are the balcony units, with beamed cathedral ceilings, private balconies, and either two queen beds or one king. The modern American decor is underlined with scenic or nature prints on the white walls. Standard units are fairly spacious and quite comfortable, with different combinations of king, queen, double, and twin beds. Even the smallest economy unit doesn't feel cramped, boasting a cabinlike decor with knotty-pine and white-stucco walls, but the views aren't quite as good as the standard and balcony units. Two family units are available.

Complimentary hot beverages are available in the mornings, and the on-site Sundeck Restaurant serves three meals daily, offering American cuisine with specialties such as fresh trout and prime rib. There's a heated outdoor pool (Memorial Day to mid-Sept) and a patio with picnic table, and the trailhead for a 0.75-mile hiking/walking trail to the visitor center at the national park is adjacent to the motel. The owners are knowledgeable hikers, and love to help with guests' hiking plans.

✪ **Aspen Lodge at Estes Park.** 6120 Colo. 7, Longs Peak Rte., Estes Park, CO 80517. ☎ **800/332-6867** (reservations only) from outside CO, or 970/586-8133. Direct from Denver ☎ **303/440-3371.** Fax 970/586-8133. www.aspenlodge.com. E-mail: aspen@aspenlodge.com. 59 units. June–Aug: 2-day minimum, packages include 3 meals, children's program, entertainment, and recreation (horseback riding extra). 2 days shared room $300 each adult, $180 each child 3–12 years, children under 3 free; single adult $380. 3 days shared room $450 each adult, $270 each child 3–12 years, children under 3 free; single adult $580. 7 days shared room $930 each adult, $610 each child 3–12 years, children under 3 free; single adult $1,345. Sept–May $79–$129 double per night for lodge units or 1-room cabins, including full breakfast. Holiday rates higher. Call for 2- and 3-room cabin rates. AE, DC, DISC, MC, V.

Among Colorado's top dude ranches, Aspen Lodge is a full-service Western-style resort, offering horseback riding, tennis, hiking, mountain biking, fishing, cross-country skiing, ice-skating, snowshoeing, and a myriad of other activities. Guests stay in the handsome log lodge, which has a commanding stone fireplace in the lobby, or in cozy one-, two-, or three-room cabins nestled among the aspens. All lodge rooms have balconies, and most rooms and cabins have splendid views of Longs Peak, the tallest mountain in Rocky Mountain National Park. Trails on the lodge's 82 acres of grounds lead directly into the national park. Guests can also enjoy an outdoor heated swimming pool and hot tub, as well as the sports center, which has racquetball, a weight room, and a sauna. Meals are varied and delicious. The lodge also schedules numerous activities to entertain both children and teens. All lodge units are nonsmoking.

✪ **Baldpate Inn.** 4900 S. Colo. 7 (P.O. Box 4445), Estes Park, CO 80517. ☎ **970/586-6151.** www.baldpateinn.com. E-mail: baldpatein@aol.com. 13 units, 4 with bathroom; 3 cabins. $85 double with shared bathroom, $100 double with private bathroom; $140 cabin. Rates include full breakfast. DISC, MC, V. Closed Nov–Apr.

Built in 1917, the Baldpate was named for the novel *Seven Keys to Baldpate,* a murder mystery in which seven visitors believe each possesses the only key to the hotel. In 1996 the Baldpate was added to the National Register of Historic Places. Guests today can watch several movie versions of the story, read the book, and add their keys to the hotel's collection of more than 20,000 keys.

Each of the early–20th-century–style rooms is unique, with handmade quilts on the beds. Several rooms are a bit small, and although most of the lodge units share bathrooms (five bathrooms for nine units), each room does have its own sink. Among our favorites are the Mae West Room (yes, she was a guest here), with a red claw-foot bathtub and wonderful views of the valley; and the Pinetop Room, which has a whirlpool tub, canopy bed, and gas fireplace. Guests can enjoy complimentary refreshments by the handsome stone fireplace in the lobby, relax on the large sundeck, or view free videos on the library VCR. But it might be difficult to stay inside, once you experience the spectacular views from the inn's spacious porch and see the nature trails beckoning. In summer, an excellent soup-and-salad buffet is served for lunch and dinner daily (see "Where to Dine," below). Smoking is not permitted.

**Big Thompson Timberlane Lodge.** 740 Moraine Ave. (P.O. Box 387), Estes Park, CO 80517. ☎ **800/898-4373** or 970/586-3137. Fax 970/586-3719. www.bigthompsontimberlanelodge.com. E-mail: bttl@peakpeak.com. 58 units. TV TEL. Summer $99–$335 per unit; off-season rates 20% to 40% lower. AE, DISC, MC, V.

You won't find more choices than at this family-oriented facility, which offers cabins, cottages, motel suites, and log homes, with sleeping for from 1 to 10 people. We especially like the cozy historic cabins for two, including several with VCRs and gas barbecue grills, that were built in the early 1900s. But there are also cabins that sleep up to six, cottages and motel units that accommodate up to six, and fully-equipped log homes of from 1,000 to 1,200 square feet that can accommodate up to 10. Cabins have knotty-pine walls, cottages have pine paneling, the motel suites have painted walls, and the log homes combine rustic-looking logs with painted walls. About half of the units have showers only (no tubs). Each unit has a refrigerator plus either a stove or a microwave. A few cabins have private hot tubs, and some have decks overlooking the river.

What makes this property especially attractive for families, in addition to family-size units, is the amenities, which include a grassy playground, outdoor heated pool and a separate wading pool for young children, a large indoor whirlpool tub (there is also a separate adults-only outdoor hot tub), picnic areas with barbecue grills, a self-serve laundry, and a stocked trout stream. A variety of toys, games, and children's books are available for kids to take to their rooms. Another plus is that it is set back from the highway, with attractively landscaped grounds.

✪ **Boulder Brook.** 1900 Fall River Rd., Estes Park, CO 80517. ☎ **800/238-0910** or 970/586-0910. Fax 970/586-8067. www.estes-park.com/boulderbrook. 16 suites. TV TEL. $89–$199 double, $129–$229 spa suites. AE, DISC, MC, V.

It would be hard to find a more beautiful setting for a lodging than this. Surrounded by tall pines, all suites face the Fall River, and all feature private riverfront decks and either full or partial kitchens. The spa suites are equipped with two-person spas, fireplaces, sitting rooms with cathedral ceilings, and king-size beds. One-bedroom suites offer king-size beds, window seats, two TVs, and bathrooms with whirlpool-tub-and-shower combinations. There's also a year-round outdoor hot tub. VCRs, in-room movies, and fax service are available, and special-occasion packages can be arranged year-round.

**Colorado Mountain School.** 351 Moraine Ave. (P.O. Box 1846), Estes Park, CO 80517. ☎ **888/267-7783** or 970/586-5758. Fax 970/586-5798. www.cmschool.com. E-mail: cmschool@cmschool.com. 18 dormitory beds. Summer $20 per bed, off-season $17. AE, DISC, MC, V. Open year-round, but office hours are 8am–5pm.

This is lodging at its simplest: coed dormitory-style rooms furnished in light woods, clean and well maintained, with bunk beds, showers, and lockable private storage. Colorado Mountain School also offers a year-round guide service and rock-climbing and mountaineering school (see "Climbing & Mountaineering," in chapter 4).

✪ **The Eagle Manor–A Bed and Breakfast Place.** 441 Chiquita Lane, Estes Park, CO 80517. ☎ **888/603-3578** (reservations) or 970/586-8482. Fax 970/586-1748. www.eaglemanor.com. E-mail: mike@eaglemanor.com or eaglemanor@estes-park.com. 4 units. TV TEL. Late May to late Sept and holidays $135 double, rest of year $125 double. Rates include full breakfast. AE, DISC, MC, V.

This Tudor-style carriage house and manor was built in 1917 by Estes Valley pioneer Frank Bond. In the 1960s a large living room with a gas fireplace, an indoor swimming pool/garden room, and additional living quarters were added. A Great Room links the old and new wings and has leather-covered overstuffed chairs and sofas. There are a wet bar with complimentary soft drinks, a wood-burning fireplace, a big-screen TV, an antique billiards table, and freshly baked cookies in the evenings. Also on premises are a sauna and an outdoor hot tub.

Rooms are spacious and comfortable. Three have queen beds and the fourth has two twins. The beds are comfortably firm and the towels are soft. The decor is a coordinated mixture of styles ranging from primitive to classic. A full breakfast of coffee, juice, eggs, breakfast meat, cereals, and breads is served in the formal dining room. Special dietary needs can be accommodated with advance notice.

Named for host Mike Smith's profession—he's a retired army colonel, or "eagle"—and personal interest in eagles, the establishment has magnificent photos of the birds by noted wildlife photographers scattered about the walls.

⭕ **Estes Park Center/YMCA of the Rockies.** 2515 Tunnel Rd., Estes Park, CO 80511-2550. ☎ **970/586-3341,** or 303/448-1616 direct from Denver. 510 lodge units, (450 with bathroom); 205 cabins. Lodge units, summer $52–$120, winter $41–$92; cabins, year-round $60–$239. YMCA membership required (available at a nominal charge). No credit cards. Pets are permitted in the cabins, but not the lodge units.

This extremely popular family resort is an ideal place to get away from it all, and serves as a great home base while exploring the Estes Park area. Lodge units are basic but perfectly adequate, and many were completely renovated in 1998. The spacious mountain cabins are equipped with two to four bedrooms (accommodating up to 10), complete kitchens, and phones; some have fireplaces. The center, which occupies 860 wooded acres, offers hiking, horseback riding, miniature golf, an indoor heated swimming pool and children's pool, fishing, bicycling (rentals available), three tennis courts, and cross-country skiing. Other facilities include conference rooms and a self-serve laundry.

**Fawn Valley Inn.** 2760 Fall River Rd. (P.O. Box 4020), Estes Park, CO 80517. ☎ **800/525-2961** or 970/586-2388. Fax 970/586-0394. www.fawnvalleyinn. com. E-mail: info@fawnvalleyinn.com. 35 units. TV TEL. Late May to mid-Sept $85–$95 motel units, $120–$175 suites and condos; rest of year $55–$65 motel units, $85–$125 suites and condos. All rates double occupancy. Minimum stay may be required at certain times. AE, DISC, MC, V.

Located only 0.5 miles from the Fall River entrance to Rocky Mountain National Park, Fawn Valley offers an attractive range of accommodations at reasonable prices. Spread across a steep bank between U.S. 34 and Fall River, each unit has a private outdoor area: deck, balcony, or patio, overlooking the river and surrounding forest-skirted mountains. The inn is often frequented by elk, deer, bighorn sheep, raccoons, and other local wildlife.

Each unit has a tub-shower combo, phone with data port, coffeemaker, and refrigerator. Most units have microwaves, and all except motel units have gas or wood-burning fireplaces. There's an outdoor heated pool (Memorial Day to Labor Day) and a hot tub. All units are spacious—even the smallest motel rooms—and have modern American decor with homey touches. The various units can accommodate from two to eight people, with king and queen beds and sofa beds. The largest condos are usually booked months in advance for summer, so call early.

**Glacier Lodge.** Colo. 66 (P.O. Box 2656), Estes Park, CO 80517. ☎ **800/ 523-3920** or 970/586-4401. www.glacierlodge.com. 28 units. TV. Early June to late Aug $95–$160, late May to early June and late Aug to late Sept $85–$130. Early to late May and late Sept through Oct $80–$98. MC, V. Closed Nov–Apr.

Deer and elk frequently visit these lovely cottages, spread across 15 wooded acres along the Big Thompson River. Poolside chalets sleep up to six; cozy, homey river duplexes with decks overlook the stream; and river triplexes range from earthy to country quaint in decor. All have porches or patios, and almost all feature kitchens and fireplaces, with firewood provided. Facilities and activities include a swimming pool, sport court, playground, fishing, gift shop, ice-cream shop, lending library, and stables. Breakfast cookouts, barbecues, and special kids' activities are held in summer, at an extra charge.

**Lake Shore Lodge.** 1700 Big Thompson Hwy., Estes Park, CO 80517. ☎ **800/332-6867** or 970/577-6400. Fax 970/577-6420. www. lakeshorelodge.com. 54 units. June–Sept $149–$179 double, $239–$279 suite; Oct–May $109–$159 double, $199–$259 suite. Rates include full breakfast. AE, DISC, MC, V.

This handsome brand-new lodge—it opened in the summer of 2000—produces a dilemma: Which do we choose, a room looking out on the lake or one with a view of the mountains? Although there are practically no lodging properties in the Estes Park area that don't have some kind of wonderful view, there are few that offer such a choice. Of course, we expect the inside to be nice, too, and the Lake Shore Lodge comes through in that category as well. Decorated in Western Victorian style, with oak furnishings and rich colors of burgundy and forest green, the rooms are slightly larger than average, and third-floor units with vaulted ceilings feel especially spacious. All units have either two queen-size beds or a king and sofa sleeper, desks, refrigerators, coffeemakers, irons and ironing boards, safes, hair dryers, two phones, data ports, and a free daily newspaper. Second- and third-floor units have decks. The six suites have fireplaces, and two also have whirlpool tubs.

Owing to its role as a conference center, the lodge has an abundance of public areas, from outdoor decks to inside sitting areas with comfortable couches, fireplaces, and, of course, great views out large windows. There's a small indoor

### *The Shining* Makes the Stanley Shine

Novelist Stephen King wrote about half of his spine-tingling novel *The Shining*—in which the caretaker of a haunted hotel goes mad—in room 217 of the Stanley Hotel. He returned in 1997 to spend 5 months at the hotel while filming the 6-hour ABC-TV miniseries.

The atmosphere of the Stanley—and its location outside Rocky Mountain National Park, where roads are closed in winter because of snow—were the impetus for King's horror novel *The Shining*. King and his wife, Tabitha, detained by bad weather, spent a night at the Stanley, and the story idea burst full-blown into his head. Signs warning of winter road closures helped reinforce his notion of being cut off from the rest of the world.

*The Shining* portrays the increasingly bizarre experiences of a caretaker's family marooned in a hotel closed for the winter. The father struggles to overcome his alcoholism while slowly going mad; his young son's supernatural powers are utilized by spirits trying to enter our physical world; and his wife provides strength, sanity, and stability in this otherwise derailed reality.

Filming the ABC miniseries at the Stanley in 1997 was King's dream come true. The actors and crew took over the entire hotel, repainting and repapering in some areas, exchanging heavy lodge-style furniture for the hotel's graceful antiques, and adding trophy animal heads to the walls to create a darker atmosphere for the imaginary Overlook Hotel.

The terrifying topiary animals gracing the front lawn of the Overlook don't exist at the Stanley—so you needn't worry that some will come to life as they did in the show. Nor will the other horrors of the film overshadow your stay. Although some people claim to see ghosts, such as a Victorian little girl who visits some rooms, the spirits at the Stanley seem to be friendly. Mementos and photos of the miniseries' filming are on display in the hotel's museum.

swimming pool and hot tub, two saunas, an exercise room, game room with video games and a pool table, and a self-serve laundry. The adjacent Lake Estes Marina offers boat rentals, and fishing is available from a boat or the lakeshore. There's a restaurant called the Silverado that serves three meals daily (see "Where to Dine," below), a lounge, and conference facilities for up to 200. All rooms are nonsmoking. Now, about the dilemma of which room to choose. The first-floor units have only limited views, so we'll eliminate those. For a standard room, the best views in our opinion are the third-floor rooms facing the lake. But, if you can afford them, the third-floor corner suites offer views of both the lake and the mountains.

**Romantic RiverSong Inn.** P.O. Box 1910, Estes Park, CO 80517. ☎ **970/586-4666.** Fax 970/577-0699. www.romanticriversong.com and www.coloradogetaways.com. E-mail: riversng@frii.com. 9 units. $150–$275 double. Rates include full breakfast. MC, V. Not suitable for small children.

Couples looking for some quiet romance while visiting Rocky Mountain National Park will enjoy this 1920 Craftsman mansion on the Big Thompson River. The elegant bed-and-breakfast has 27 forested acres with hiking trails and a trout pond, as well as prolific wildlife and beautiful wildflowers. Very quiet, the inn is at the end of a country lane, the first right off Mary's Lake Road after it branches off U.S. 36 south. The comfortable bedrooms are decorated with a blend of antique and modern country furniture, and all have fireplaces. Some feature ornate brass beds and claw-foot tubs, and several boast jet tubs for two. Innkeeper Gary Mansfield, a mail-order minister, conducts weddings at the inn, or, for the athletically inclined, on snowshoe treks into the national park. Gourmet candlelight dinners are available by advance arrangement ($69 per couple), but you must supply your own alcoholic beverages. Smoking is not permitted.

**Stanley Hotel.** 333 Wonderview Ave. (P.O. Box 1767), Estes Park, CO 80517. ☎ **800/976-1377** or 970/586-3371. Fax 970/586-3673. www.stanhot@ix. Netcom.com. 135 units. TV TEL. Late May to mid-Oct $159–$209 double, $269–$299 suite; mid-Oct to late May $129–$179 double, $219–$249 suite. AE, DISC, MC, V.

Fans of the automotive, the historic, and the horrific should check out a stay at this hotel. F. O. Stanley, inventor of the Stanley Steam Car, opened this elegant, white-pillared hotel in 1909. The hotel, listed in the National Register of Historic Places, was built into solid rock and ran entirely on electric power—including the kitchen. Stanley built a hydroelectric plant and water system to provide power and running water for both the hotel and Estes Park. Heat was the only thing the resort lacked back then, but happily that problem was remedied in 1979. The hotel has also gained fame as the inspiration for Stephen King's masterpiece of horror, *The Shining* (See "*The Shining* Makes the Stanley Shine," above).

The entire building, both guest rooms and public areas, was remodeled in 1997. As is often the case in historic hotels, the rooms differ in size and shape, and offer a variety of views of Longs Peak, Lake Estes, and surrounding hillsides. We prefer the deluxe rooms in the front of the hotel that provide views into the national park. Furnishings are in keeping with the building's Georgian architecture, with 1920s-era mahogany pieces—some original and many reproductions. Amenities include a heated outdoor pool, tennis and volleyball courts, a sundeck, access to a nearby health club, shops, and a business center. And, of course, there's a vintage Stanley Steamer in the lobby.

The hotel has two restaurants: The MacGregor Room serves continental cuisine with a Louisiana flair (dinner prices range from $19 to $40), and the less formal Cascades serves American cuisine and offers live entertainment Friday and Saturday evenings. All baked goods are prepared fresh daily by the pastry chef. The hotel also has a gift shop and a museum (see "What to See & Do," above), and tours of the hotel and museum are available by appointment (☎ **970/577-1903**).

**Streamside Cabins.** 1260 Fall River Rd., Moraine Rte. (P.O. Box 2930), Estes Park, CO 80517. ☎ **800/321-3303** or 970/586-6464. Fax 970/586-6272. www.streamsidecabins.com. E-mail: resv@streamsidecabins.com. 19 units. TV. Late Oct to early May $75–$145 double, early May to late Oct $95–$225 double. AE, DISC, MC, V.

Everything is top-drawer at these cabin suites, set on 17 acres along the Fall River, about a mile west of Estes Park on U.S. 34, and surrounded by woods and meadows rife with wildflowers. Deer, elk, and the occasional bighorn sheep are such regular visitors that many have been given names.

The solid-wood cabins are furnished like condominiums, and equipped with king or queen beds, fireplaces, VCRs, and decks or patios with gas grills. Most feature full kitchens, cathedral ceilings, skylights, and whirlpool tubs or steam showers. Guests can also use an indoor hot tub/swim spa and hike the nature trails. A variety of special-occasion packages are offered.

## WHERE TO DINE

You'll find a wide variety of places to eat in Estes Park, ranging from fast-food joints to several excellent fine-dining establishments and a number of restaurants offering good,
wholesome food at reasonable prices. The town is a base camp
for hikers and many active people, and the portions at most
restaurants we visited seemed larger than average; so those
with smaller appetites may want to ask about half portions.
One way to cut expenses is to pick up picnic supplies or deli
sandwiches at a local supermarket. In addition to the stores
listed under "Supplies," under "Fast Facts: Rocky Mountain
National Park," in chapter 3, you'll find a deli, a large produce
section, and a complete selection of groceries at **Safeway,**
451 E. Wonderview Ave., in Stanley Village Center (☎ **970/
586-4447**).

In addition to the following choices, we recommend the
**Lazy B Ranch,** 1915 Dry Gulch Rd. (☎ **800/228-2116** or
970/586-5371), which serves a chuck-wagon supper with a
show of live Western music and comedy. There's also a program on the history of Western music. Cost is $15 for anyone
13 or older, $12 for those 10 to 12 years old, and $8 for children under 10. To get to Lazy B, take U.S. 34 east from Estes
Park about 1½ miles, turn left at Sombrero Stables, and follow the signs. The ranch is open from late May through September, but the schedule varies, so call for specific times and
days.

✪ **Andrea's of Estes.** 145 E. Elkhorn Ave. ☎ **970/586-0886.** Reservations
suggested for dinner, not accepted at lunch. Lunch $5.50–$10, dinner $6–$24.
AE, DC, DISC, MC, V. Wed–Mon 11am–9pm, Fri–Sat 11am–10pm.
CONTINENTAL.

Andrea's offers fine dining in a pleasant modern European
atmosphere, and a rooftop deck, open from mid-April
through September, that provides the best view of striking
Longs Peak from anywhere downtown. The carpeted dining
room has an intimate feel, with light-wood bar and accents.
The lunch menu offers soup, salads, and sandwiches—including a buffalo burger and veggie burger; plus fish and chips,
BBQ ribs, and Rocky Mountain trout. At dinner, the most
popular items are fresh Rocky Mountain pan-fried trout with
lemon pepper and piñon nuts and served with rice, and elk
medallions smothered with a rich red-wine reduction sauce

and served with spätzle. Other dinner choices include several classic Italian dishes, German specialties such as Wiener or Holstein schnitzel, beef or buffalo steaks, and barbecued baby back ribs. All baking is done on premises, with specialty desserts created daily. A children's menu is available.

**Aspen Lodge Dining Room.** At the Aspen Lodge, 6120 Colo. 7, Longs Peak Route, about 8 miles south of Estes Park. ☎ **970/586-8133.** Reservations recommended. Lunch $6–$9, dinner $14–$22. AE, DC, DISC, MC, V. Daily 7–9:30am, noon–2pm, and 6–9pm. WESTERN/CONTINENTAL.

Enjoy casually elegant dining in this large room, which features a cathedral ceiling, wagon wheel chandeliers, and Western artwork. Broad windows provide unfettered views of the grand outdoors: a small lake in front, evergreen and deciduous trees on the sloping grounds, and the Rocky Mountains. For lunch there are burgers, sandwiches, chicken-fried steak, Rocky Mountain trout, and fried chicken. Dinners include a salad bar, fresh rolls, the crisp and tender vegetable du jour, and a potato or rice. Popular entrees include the farmhouse chicken—a fresh boneless breast stuffed with smoked ham and Monterey jack cheese, and baked with Parmesan and Romano cheeses before being finished with a mushroom Marsala demiglaze; and low-fat grilled buffalo smothered with grilled onion and peppers. The menu also offers pastas, steaks, seafood, prime rib, and a variety of decadent desserts.

✪ **Baldpate Inn.** 4900 S. Colo. 7. ☎ **970/586-6151.** Reservations recommended. Buffet $10.75 adults, $8.25 children under 10. DISC, MC, V. Memorial Day through Sept daily 11:30am–8pm. SOUP & SALAD.

Don't be misled by the simple cuisine here—the buffet is deliciously filling and plentiful. Everything is freshly made on the premises, and the cooks barely stay one muffin pan ahead of the guests. Soups include hearty stews, chili, a marvelous chicken rice, a garden vegetable, and a classic French onion, with a choice of two offered each day. The salad bar provides fresh greens and an array of toppings, chunks of cheese, and fruit and vegetable salads. Honey wheat bread is a staple, and there are wonderful rolls, muffins, and corn bread. To top off the meal there are fresh homemade pies and cappuccino. The Baldpate, on the National Register of Historic Places, is entirely nonsmoking. See also "Where to Stay," above.

**Bob and Tony's Pizza.** 124 W. Elkhorn Ave. ☎ **970/586-2044.** Sa. and meals $5–$7.50, whole pizzas $9–$23.50. AE, DISC, MC, V. Summe 11am–10pm, shorter hours the rest of the year. PIZZA.

This busy and somewhat noisy locally owned and operated pizza joint is what we think a pizza place should be—redbrick walls covered with chalk signatures, a large stone fireplace with chairs for those waiting for their to-go pies, and utilitarian tables. The pizza dough, sauce, and Italian sausage are made fresh in-house from family recipes. A variety of pizzas are offered, or you can "build your own" from a wide choice of toppings, although why anyone would want to put sauerkraut on a pizza is beyond our comprehension! Sandwiches range from Italian sausage to French dip to grilled chicken, and there are also "build your own" subs, and meals such as fish, fries, and slaw; spaghetti with meatballs; and even Rocky Mountain oysters with fries. There's also a soup-and-salad bar.

✪ **The Dunraven Inn.** 2470 Colo. 66. ☎ **970/586-6409.** Reservations highly recommended. Main courses $7–$32. AE, DISC, MC, V. Sun–Thurs 5–10pm, Fri–Sat 5–11pm. Closes slightly earlier in winter. ITALIAN.

Images of the *Mona Lisa* are scattered about, from a mustachioed lady to opera posters, and autographed dollar bills are posted in the lounge area. House specialties include scampi; linguini with white clam sauce; veal parmigiana; chicken cacciatore; and Dunraven Italiano, a charbroiled sirloin steak in a sauce of green, red, and yellow peppers, with black olives, mushrooms, and tomatoes. There's a wide choice of pasta, fresh seafood, vegetarian plates, and desserts, and a children's menu is offered.

**Ed's Cantina & Grill.** 362 E. Elkhorn Ave. ☎ **970/586-2919.** Lunch and dinner main courses $4.95–$9.95. AE, MC, V. Daily from 7am through dinner. MEXICAN.

The first thing you'll notice is the wide use of the chili motif, and next will be the long wooden bar and neon signs. Naturally, chilies play an important role in the food. Feast on huevos rancheros and a breakfast burrito; quesadilla, taco salad, green-chili burgers; or combination plates, fajitas, burritos. Those preferring less spicy fare can select from plenty of traditional egg and pancake plates, sandwiches, soups, salads, burgers, and roasted chicken. Everything on Ed's extensive menu is also available for takeout.

lkhorn at the corner of U.S. Highways 34 and 36. courses $3.95–$7.95. AE, DC, DISC, MC, V. Sum- un 7am–2pm; winter daily 7am–2pm. AMERICAN.

place to start your day, the Egg & I is deco- ..... earth tones, with magnificent views of the pristine Rocky Mountains. Breakfast is available at any time, ranging from the simplest fried egg to several variations of eggs Benedict, omelets, frittatas, crepes, skillet meals—and we do mean meals—plus pancakes and French toast. Those not opting for breakfast can choose among a variety of sandwiches, such as the California croissant, thinly sliced turkey breast, Swiss cheese, alfalfa sprouts, tomato, and avocado on a fresh tender croissant. Soups and a number of salads are also available, and there is takeout. Nonsmoking.

**Estes Park Brewery.** 470 Prospect Village Dr. ☎ **970/586-5421.** Sandwiches and salads $4.95–$6.95, dinner main courses $9.95–$15.95. AE, CB, DC, DISC, MC, V. Summer daily 11am–midnight; closes earlier in winter. AMERICAN.

Pizzas, burgers, sandwiches—including meatball and grilled turkey—and bratwurst made with the brewery's own beer are the fare here. Vegetarians can order a veggie burger and a variety of salads; kids have their own menu. In addition, a number of full dinners are also offered, ranging from barbecued chicken to Rocky Mountain rainbow trout to steak. The brewery offers about 10 fresh beers at any given time, specializing in Belgian-style ales. It also produces an excellent India pale ale and an especially pleasant stout. Even children are welcome in the tasting room, where they can sample the brewery's own root beer and cream soda—on tap, of course.

**Grumpy Gringo.** 1560 Big Thompson Ave. (U.S. 34). ☎ **970/586-7705.** www.grumpygringo.com. Main courses $5–$15. AE, DISC, MC, V. Summer daily 11am–10pm; slightly shorter hours in winter. Closed last week of Jan and first week of Feb. On U.S. 34, 1 mile east of the junction of U.S. Highways 34 and 36. MEXICAN.

Dine in style at this classy Mexican restaurant without breaking your bank. The private booths, whitewashed plaster walls, green plants and paper poppies for a splash of color, and a few choice sculptures provide an atmosphere usually associated with high-cost dining. And although the food is excellent and portions are large, the prices are surprisingly low. Choose from several different burritos, or order the enchilada olé, a mammoth made up of three different enchiladas: cheese, beef, and chicken. The fajitas—either chicken or beef—are delicious. There are six sauces to choose from, each homemade and rated mild, semihot, or hot. Burgers and sandwiches are also offered, and there's a children's menu. The house specialty drink is the Gringo Margarita—made with José Cuervo gold tequila from an original (and secret) recipe. The full bar also offers frozen fruit margaritas, about a dozen premium tequilas, a good selection of beer—including Mexican—and wine.

✪ **Molly B.** 200 Moraine Ave. ☎ **970/586-2766.** Reservations recommended for dinner. Main courses $3–$7 breakfast, $5–$8 lunch, $8–$17 dinner. AE, MC, V. Thurs–Tues 6:30am–3pm year-round; plus 4–9pm May–Oct. AMERICAN.

The friendly staff makes you feel right at home in this busy, casual restaurant, which, along with the freshly prepared home-style food, makes this a must-stop for us when we're in Estes Park. Located in an older building, the dining room has light-colored pine walls and tables that help provide a down-home atmosphere. It's especially popular at breakfast, with specialties such as the sunrise stuffer—a large tortilla filled with scrambled eggs, potatoes, cheese, and spicy chorizo. Lunch and dinner selections include vegetarian entrees, fresh seafood, pasta, prime rib, and steak. Desserts are made in-house, and full liquor service was recently added. Patio seating, providing good people-watching along the noisy street, is available in warm weather.

**Silverado.** At Lake Shore Lodge, 1700 Big Thompson Hwy. ☎ **970/577-6400.** www.lakeshorelodge.com. Reservations recommended for dinner in summer. Main courses $5.95–$10.95 lunch, $10.95–$24.95 dinner. AE, DISC, MC, V. Daily 7am–2pm and 5–10pm. STEAK/SEAFOOD.

In keeping with the rest of this hotel and conference facility, the restaurant at the Lake Shore Lodge boasts wonderful views, both of Lake Estes and out at the mountains in Rocky Mountain National Park. The dining room, of massive log post-and-beam construction, is simply but tastefully decorated in a Western theme, with upholstered wood chairs, wood tables, and a gas-fired fireplace. Dinner entrees are the way we like them—top-quality meat and fish, carefully prepared with only limited use of sauces. We especially like the grilled 10-ounce buffalo rib-eye and the slow-roasted prime rib, served au jus. But for those seeking a bit more excitement, we also suggest the 14-ounce New York strip served with a Jack Daniels sauce. There are also several chicken dishes and our fish choice, Rocky Mountain trout sautéed and flambéed with Amaretto and sliced almonds. The lunch menu offers a good selection of salads and sandwiches, and breakfast (included in room rates for guests, $7.95 for others) is an extensive hot buffet. Patio dining is available in good weather. The dining room is nonsmoking.

**Timberline Family Restaurant.** 451 S. St. Vrain Ave. ☎ **970/586-9840.** Sun brunch $4.50–$12, dinner main courses $6.50–$21. AE, DISC, MC, V. Sun brunch 10am–2pm; dinner daily 4–10pm. AMERICAN.

Friendly service and good home-style cooking are the hallmarks of the Timberline. The pleasant, light-pine–paneled dining room has a mountain-lodge decor, complete with a moss rock fireplace, local and regional artwork, and three-dimensional petroglyphlike figures. For dinner we particularly recommend the Rocky Mountain trout, one of the charbroiled steaks, or the coconut shrimp served with a spicy marmalade sauce. The menu also includes American standards such as liver and onions and Western favorites like chicken-fried steak. A local favorite is the Timberline salad—a mixture of fresh garden greens topped with mandarin orange, pear slices, and Parmesan cheese, and served with raspberry vinaigrette dressing. Grilled chicken can be added to the salad if you like. Among homemade desserts, we suggest the coconut cream pie. The popular Sunday brunch offers a good selection of breakfast and lunch items, including omelets, eggs Benedict, fried chicken, and grilled salmon. The entire property is nonsmoking.

## 2  Grand Lake

108 miles NW of Denver, 49 miles W of Estes Park (road open only in summer), 14 miles N of Granby, 93 miles E of Steamboat Springs

The western entrance to Rocky Mountain National Park is at the picturesque little town of Grand Lake, which lies in the shade of Shadow Mountain at the park's southwestern corner. If you're coming from Steamboat Springs or Glenwood Springs, Grand Lake is a convenient base from which to explore the park. You can get there at any time of year, via U.S. Highways 40 and 34. In summer, you can also get to

Grand Lake by taking Trail Ridge Road through Rocky Mountain National Park from Estes Park. Both routes are scenic, although the national-park route (closed by snow in winter) is definitely prettier.

Grand Lake is smaller and quieter than Estes Park, and it affords easy access to three beautiful lakes that are practically at your doorstep, and to the numerous trailheads into the surrounding national forest. There are several attractive historic lodgings near Grand Lake, and some good dining choices.

Here, in the crisp mountain air at 8,370 feet above sea level, you can stroll down an old-fashioned boardwalk while a local resident on horseback parallels you on Grand Avenue. Surrounded by Shadow Mountain Lake, Grand Lake, the Arapaho National Recreation Area, and Rocky Mountain National Park, the community of Grand Lake offers numerous activities for the outdoor enthusiast. Both lakes, and nearby Lake Granby, have marinas that offer boating (with rentals), fishing, and other water sports. Throughout the recreation area and the surrounding national forests, you'll find miles of trails for hiking, horseback riding, four-wheeling, and mountain biking that become cross-country skiing and snowmobiling trails in winter.

## ESSENTIALS

**VISITOR INFORMATION**   For a complete listing of lodging and dining choices in the Grand Lake Area, contact the **Grand Lake Area Chamber of Commerce,** P.O. Box 57, Grand Lake, CO 80447 (☎ **800/531-1019** or 970/627-3372; fax 970/627-8007; www.grandlakechamber.com; e-mail: glinfo@grandlakechamber.com). The chamber operates a visitor center (☎ **970/627-3402**) at the Y junction of U.S. 34 and the road into town.

**PICNICKING/CAMPING SUPPLIES**   The **Mountain Food Market** and the **Circle D,** 701 Grand Ave. (☎ **970/627-3210**), have good selections of groceries and picnic supplies. Picnic and fishing supplies can be found at **Grand Lake Pharmacy.** For more information, see "Fast Facts: Rocky Mountain National Park," in chapter 3, and "Camper Services & Supplies," in chapter 5.

**CALENDAR OF EVENTS**   Snowmobile Racing, early January; Winter Carnival, late January; Grand Lake High-Altitude Sled-Dog Championships, late February to early March;

Granby Ice-Fishing Derby, late February or early March; Grand Spring Fishing Derby, mid-May; Fourth of July fireworks over the lake; Buffalo Barbecue Celebration and Parade, mid-July; Grand Lake Regatta and Lipton Cup Races, late July or early August; Old-Fashioned Christmas Yuletide Celebration, mid-December through New Year's.

## GETTING OUTDOORS

The town of Grand Lake rests in the elbow of Grand Lake (called "Spirit Lake" by the Arapaho) and Shadow Mountain Lake. Rocky Mountain National Park, the Arapaho National Forest, and Arapaho National Recreation Area encircle the town, and when you factor in the surrounding water and wilderness, the town is teeming with opportunities for outdoor adventures. The activities and businesses found in the immediate Grand Lake vicinity are listed below. See below for specifics on the national forest and recreation area.

**BICYCLING**    For rentals, maps, and repairs, stop at **Rocky Mountain Sports,** 830 Grand Ave. (☎ **970/627-8124**). This full-service bicycle shop, which calls itself the "home of the French Wrench," boasts certified mechanics and clerks and repair people fluent in English, French, Spanish, and Italian. Call for current rental rates and availability.

**BOATING**    The area's three lakes provide plenty of opportunities for boating and other water sports. Grand Lake has a boat ramp on its east end, and there are public piers, a public beach, and two private marinas on its north shore. For rentals and lake cruises, stop at **Boaters Choice,** 1246 Lake Ave. (at the east end of Grand Avenue, turn right for a block to Lake Avenue; ☎ **970/627-9273**). A 45-minute cruise costs $9 for adults and $5 for children; one child under 10 with a paying adult rides free. Cruises depart at 1pm Monday to Thursday, and at 11am and 2pm on Friday and Saturday. Rentals start at $13 an hour for canoes, $20 an hour for a small boat with an outboard motor, and $56 an hour for a pontoon boat with a 10-person capacity.

A canal connects Grand Lake and Shadow Mountain Lake. At Shadow Mountain Lake, **Trail Ridge Marina** (☎ **970/627-3586**) offers boat rentals at similar rates to Boaters Choice. Also see "Boating," in "Arapaho National Forest & National Recreation Area," below.

For personal watercraft, stop at **Spirit Lake Rentals,** 347 Grand Avenue (☎ **800/894-3336** or 970/627-9288; www.spiritlakerentals.com; e-mail: slpolaris@coweblink.net). Rentals start at $60 per hour and include a life vest; wet-suit rental costs $5 per day. Launching and pickup services on Grand Lake are offered for an extra fee.

The Grand Lake Yacht Club hosts the **Grand Lake Regatta** and **Lipton Cup Races** each summer in late July or early August. The club was organized in 1902, and the regatta began 10 years later. Sailboats from around the world compete to win the prestigious Lipton Cup, given to the club by Thomas Lipton in 1912.

**FISHING**   Anglers can try for rainbow, lake, and brown trout in the 500-acre, 226-foot-deep Grand Lake. Although some large (20-lb.) lake trout are still occasionally caught, heavy fishing has taken its toll on the population, so stocking has been resumed. Rainbow trout are also stocked in summer. Two handicapped-accessible fishing areas are located on the lake's west and east shores.

**GOLFING**   Test your golfing skills at the 18-hole, par-74 championship **Grand Lake Golf Course,** 1415 County Rd. 48 (☎ **970/627-8008**), at an altitude of 8,420 feet. The greens fee for 9 holes is $30, and for 18 holes it's $55; and there are a pro shop and a restaurant on the premises.

**OFF-ROADING**   Stop at **Spirit Lake Rentals** (see "Boating," above) for an ATV or four-wheel-drive jeep you can use to motor out into the high mountains around Grand Lake. A Polaris 250 Trail Boss starts at $90 for 4 hours (includes safety training, trailer, gas, and helmet), and you must have a vehicle with a trailer hitch. Jeep rentals start at about $70 for 2 hours.

**RAFTING**   To experience the excitement of white water, contact **Mad Adventures,** P.O. Box 650, Winter Park, CO 80482 (☎ **800/451-4844** or 970/726-5290). The company offers a range of excursions, including mild float trips on the Colorado River. A half-day trip costs $36 for adults and $32 for children; a full-day trip costs $55 and $45, respectively. Also see "Rafting," in "Roosevelt National Forest," below.

**SNOWMOBILING**   Snowmobile enthusiasts can head into the mountains on their own if they stop in at **Spirit Lake Rentals** (see "Boating," above). Polaris snowmobile rentals range from $60 to $90 for 2 hours, depending on the type of snowmobile, and a trailer is not needed because you start your snowmobile trip from the rental shop. Rates include a tank of gas, oil, a helmet, snowmobile clothing, and a trail map.

Ski-Doo snowmobiles are available at **Lone Eagle Rentals,** 720 Grand Ave. (☎ **800/282-3311** or 970/627-3310), starting at $70 for two people for 2 hours. Rentals include suits, helmets, boots, gas, oil, and map.

## WHAT TO SEE & DO

**Kauffman House.** 407 Pitkin Ave. ☎ **970/627-3351.** Admission free, donations welcome. Daily 11am–5pm. Closed Labor Day to Memorial Day.

Log-cabin and history enthusiasts will enjoy a visit to this museum of pioneer memorabilia. The log house was originally built by Ezra Kauffman in 1892 as a hotel. Cutting and shaping the logs by hand, Kauffman first built a square two-story structure, and later added a kitchen, a parlor, and five additional bedrooms. He ran the hotel until his death in 1921, and his widow and daughters continued the operation until World War II. The Grand Lake Historical Society was formed in 1973 to restore and preserve the house, and it is now listed on the National Register of Historic Places.

## WHERE TO STAY

There are plenty of lodging possibilities in the Grand Lake area. In addition to the properties discussed below, private homes can be rented for nightly, weekly, or monthly stays through **Grand Lake Reservations,** P.O. Box 1211, Grand Lake, CO 80447 (☎ **800/800-6096** or 970/627-8772; www.co-biz.com/grandlakereservations). Air-conditioning is almost never needed at this elevation.

**Bighorn Lodge Best Value Inn.** 613 Grand Ave. (P.O. Box 1760), Grand Lake, CO 80477. ☎ **800/341-8000** or 970/627-8101. www.rkymtnhi.com/ bighorn. E-mail: bighorn@rkymtnhi.com. 20 units. TV TEL. Summer and holidays $70–$130 double, rest of year $55–$70 double. AE, CB, DC, DISC, MC, V.

Located just 3 blocks from the center of downtown, the Bighorn Lodge offers well-maintained modern motel rooms with one or two queen beds, a table and two upholstered chairs, ceiling fans, and a vanity separate from the bathrooms, which have tub-shower combos. Some units have a refrigerator and microwave, and complimentary hot beverages are available in the lobby. The town's namesake lake is 4 blocks south of the lodge.

**☉ Daven Haven Lodge.** 604 Marina Dr. (P.O. Box 1528), Grand Lake, CO 80447. ☎ **970/627-8144.** Fax 970/627-5098. www.grandlakecolorado. com/dh. E-mail: davenhaven@rkymtnhi.com. 16 cabins. TV. $78–$185 double. Off-season midweek discounts available. 3-night minimum required on reservations mid-June to Labor Day and holidays. DISC, MC, V.

Those seeking seclusion and quiet in a mountain-resort setting will find happiness at this group of cabins, set among pine trees about 1 block from the lake. The lobby has a stone fireplace, some old Coke machines, and several antique jukeboxes—they actually play 78-RPM records! The cabins vary in size, sleeping from two to nine people; each has its own picnic table and six have stone fireplaces. Decor and furnishings vary, but most have attractive light-wood walls and both solid-wood and upholstered furniture. You'll also find a heated swimming pool (open in summer), a volleyball court, horseshoes, a bonfire pit, and a barbecue area. Complimentary morning coffee is served in summer. The Back-Street Steakhouse (see "Where to Dine," below) is open for dinner in summer.

**Driftwood Lodge.** 12255 U.S. 34 (P.O. Box 609), Grand Lake, CO 80447. ☎ and fax **970/627-3654.** www.rkymtnhi.com/driftwood. E-mail: jsig@ rkymtnhi.com. 17 units. TV TEL. Summer $70–$85 double, $95 suites; lower rates in winter. DISC, MC, V.

Located 3 miles south of town across from Shadow Mountain Lake, this comfortable and well-maintained establishment is a great bet if all you're looking for is a basic motel room or suite. It has a swimming pool, sauna, whirlpool, and playground.

**E.G.'s Garden Grill & Country Inn.** 1000 Grand Ave. (P.O. Box 1618), Grand Lake, CO 80447. ☎ **970/627-8404.** Fax 970/627-0118. 3 units. TV TEL. $110–$145 double. Rates include full breakfast. AE, DISC, MC, V.

Located in downtown Grand Lake on the third floor of a 1910 building, this bed-and-breakfast is a good choice for those seeking a bit more personal attention than will be found in the area's standard motels and larger lodges. The three spacious, well-appointed rooms are individually decorated and have some antiques. Each has a whirlpool tub, a gas fireplace, combination TV/VCR unit, and one queen- or king-size bed. For a room with a view, you can't do much better than this: two rooms overlook the lake, and the third faces the national park.

Room service for lunch and dinner is available from E.G.'s Garden Grill downstairs (see "Where to Dine," below), and the full breakfast is delivered to your room each morning. All rooms are nonsmoking.

✪ **Grand Lake Lodge.** 15500 U.S. 34 (P.O. Box 569), Grand Lake, CO 80447. ☎ **970/627-3967.** Fax 970/627-9495. www.grandlakelodge.com. 56 units. $70–$160 double. Minimum stays apply to most units, and all units on weekends and holidays. AE, DISC, MC, V. Closed mid-Sept through May. Take U.S. 34 north 0.5 miles from Grand Lake (or 0.5 miles south of the park entrance) and turn east (watch for their sign) onto the entrance road.

At an elevation of 8,769 feet, Grand lake Lodge brags about having Colorado's "favorite front porch," and we have to admit that the lodge's veranda offers spectacular panoramic views of Grand Lake—both the town and the lake—and the surrounding mountains. Established in 1921, the Lodge has been owned and operated by three generations of the Ted L. James family since 1953. It offers excellent service and food in a delightful rustic setting, with sleeping quarters in modern cabins scattered among the pines beyond the Main Lodge.

Decor and furnishings vary, but most have Southwest-style bed coverings and upholstery, and walls of wood-grain paneling. Units range from single rooms (that sleep two) in a duplex cabin, to two rooms with fully equipped kitchenettes and either gas heat or a Franklin stove (these units sleep four to six). There's a large outdoor heated pool, hot tub, decks, playground, picnic area with grills, riding stables, volleyball, horseshoes, and hiking trails; recreation room with games, Ping-Pong, pool table, and laundry facilities; a large gift shop, a bar, and a restaurant (see "Where to Dine," below).

**The Inn at Grand Lake.** 1103 Grand Ave. (P.O. Box 1590), Grand Lake, CO 80447. ☎ **800/722-2585** or 970/627-9234. 17 units. TV TEL. $60–$70 double; 10% to 20% less in spring and fall. DISC, MC, V.

For modern lodging with an Old West feel, stay at this restored historic building, originally built in 1881 as Grand Lake's courthouse and jail. Rooms have a variety of bed combinations, and several sleep up to six. They're equipped with Western-style furniture, have ceiling fans, white stucco walls, and Indian-motif draperies and bedspreads. Over half the units have refrigerators and microwaves. About half of the units have shower-tub combinations, and the rest have showers only. The best views are on the street side of the building.

The inn is located in the center of town, about a half block from the lake.

**Western Riviera Motel.** 419 Garfield Ave. (P.O. Box 1286), Grand Lake, CO 80447. ☎ **970/627-3580.** Fax 970/627-3320. www.westernriv.com. 15 units. TV TEL. $90–$110 double summer and holidays; other times 10% to 20% less. AE, MC, V.

Located on the north shore of Grand Lake, the Western Riviera offers spacious basic rooms plus suites that sleep up to six. All are clean, comfortable, and well maintained, with enticing views of the lake. The suites have refrigerators, and the motel has an outdoor hot tub.

## WHERE TO DINE

**A.M. Breakfast.** 725 Grand Ave. ☎ **970/627-8312.** Reservations not accepted for breakfast; required for dinner. Breakfast $2.95–$6.95, dinner $6.50–$14.50 (half price for children under 12). AE, DISC, MC, V. Summer Thurs–Tues 7am–12:30pm, winter Fri–Tues 7am–12:30pm; year-round Fri–Tues 5pm–close. The restaurant may close for a week or 2 each Nov and Apr. AMERICAN/CONTINENTAL.

A large fieldstone fireplace on one wall dominates this small casual restaurant, a local favorite for breakfast and dinner fondues. The rough, cream-painted plaster walls provide the background for a large mural of Grand Lake that sits across from three large windows welcoming the morning sun. Service is fast and friendly, and you'll find all the usual breakfast favorites plus a quiche of the day, a breakfast burrito, and daily specials. The dinner menu offers a variety of tasty fondues, including one with pasta. People who are very sensitive to cigarette smoke may want to stay away, because there is no non-smoking section.

**Back-Street Steakhouse.** In the Daven Haven Lodge, 604 Marina Dr. ☎ **970/627-8144.** Reservations recommended in summer and on winter weekends. Main courses $14–$28. DISC, MC, V. Summer and Christmas holidays Sun–Fri 5–9pm, Sat 5–10pm; winter Wed–Sat 5–9pm. Closed Nov and Apr. STEAKS.

This cozy, country-inn–like restaurant offers fine dining in a down-home atmosphere. Steaks—from the 8-ounce filet mignon to the 20-ounce porterhouse—are all USDA choice beef, cooked to perfection. The house specialty, Jack Daniel's pork chops (breaded, baked, and served with a creamy Jack Daniel's mushroom sauce), was featured in *Bon Appétit* magazine. Also on the menu are pasta, chicken, and fish dishes, plus slow-roasted prime rib, and children's items.

**Chuck Hole Cafe.** 1131 Grand Ave. ☎ **970/627-3509.** Main courses $2.95–$6.25. No credit cards. Daily 7am–2pm. AMERICAN.

Eat traditional fare while surrounded by historic photos and prints at this small cafe. The place has a Western atmosphere and serves breakfast items such as omelets and pancakes, and quick lunches including burgers and deli-style sandwiches.

✪ **E.G.'s Garden Grill.** 1000 Grand Ave. ☎ **970/627-8404.** Main courses $7–$11.50 lunch, $8–$25 dinner. AE, DISC, MC, V. Summer daily 11am–10pm; call for winter hours. NEW AMERICAN/SOUTHWESTERN.

If you want to try innovative American cuisine served in a congenial setting, it would be hard to top this eatery. The large stone fireplace, trellised ceiling, and spacious outdoor beer garden give this restaurant a warm and comfortable atmosphere. The menu offers creative variations on traditional American dishes, often with a Southwestern flair. Although the menu changes seasonally, house specialties usually include items such as mustard catfish with jalapeño tartar sauce and jicama slaw, shrimp enchiladas, tortilla-crusted ruby red trout, and Barb's baby back ribs with E.G.'s homemade BBQ sauce. Pizza, sandwiches, soups and salads, daily seafood specials, and a children's menu are available. There's also a fairly extensive wine list.

**Grand Lake Lodge Restaurant.** 15500 U.S. 34. ☎ **970/627-3967.** Reservations required for dinner and brunch. Main courses $5.95–$8.25 lunch, $13–$21 dinner. AE, DISC, MC, V. Mon–Sat 7:30–10am and 11:30am–2:30pm, Sun brunch 9:30am–1:30pm; dinner daily from 5:30pm. Closed mid-Sept through May. Take U.S. 34 north 0.5 miles from Grand Lake (or 0.5 miles south of the park entrance) and turn east (watch for their sign) onto the entrance road. AMERICAN.

Come here to enjoy a lunch on the sunny front porch (see "Where to Stay," above) overlooking Grand Lake and Shadow Mountain Reservoir. The lunch menu includes soups and salads, favorites such as buffalo or beef burgers, and grilled rainbow trout. For dinner you might try one of the nightly fish and game specials or one of the signature dishes, such as sautéed pork medaillons with crabmeat and wild mushrooms or the steak au poivre with brandy peppercorn sauce. All desserts are baked in-house. Afternoon appetizers are available in the bar from 2:30 to 5pm daily, and there is live musical entertainment from 9:30pm to 12:30am nightly.

**Marie's Grand Lake Cafe.** 928 Grand Ave. ☎ **970/627-9475.** Lunch $3.50–$6.50, dinner $5.50–$16. AE, DISC, MC, V. Summer daily 6am–10pm; slightly shorter hours in winter. AMERICAN.

Nostalgia buffs will enjoy the counter at this large corner cafe, which has the feel of a 1950s diner. This is our pick for breakfast—the choice is extensive—which is served until 2pm. Daily specials are offered at every meal. There are soups and salads, burgers, plus croissant and regular sandwiches available for lunch. Although they're not exactly low-cholesterol, we recommend the steak and eggs for breakfast and chicken-fried steak for dinner. Also on the dinner menu are homemade meat loaf, roast beef, fish and chips, and several Mexican dishes such as burritos, tacos, fajitas, and enchiladas. We also like the pies, which are baked in-house.

## 3  Roosevelt National Forest

Named for President Theodore Roosevelt, who is credited with creating the national-forest system, the 1,240-square-mile Roosevelt National Forest offers numerous opportunities for hiking, mountain biking, four-wheeling, fishing, and camping. It extends southward from the Wyoming state line, wrapping around the northern, eastern, and southern boundaries of Rocky Mountain National Park and the community of Estes Park, and butts up against the Arapaho National Forest, which runs along the west side of the national park. Roosevelt National Forest includes the Cache la Poudre (*Poo*-der) Wild and Scenic River, has several designated wilderness areas, and offers almost unlimited opportunities for hiking, mountain biking, horseback riding, fishing, and camping (see chapter 5). Unlike in the national parks, national-forest regulations generally permit leashed dogs on trails, and, except in designated wilderness areas, mountain bikes are also permitted on many trails.

### ESSENTIALS

**INFORMATION & VISITOR CENTER** For information, contact the **Forest Service Information Center,** 1311 S. College Ave., Fort Collins, CO 80524 (☎ **970/498-2770**). There is also a **Forest Service Information Center** in Estes Park, at 161 Second St. (☎ **970/586-3440**); it's open daily from 9am to 5pm in summer, and from 9am to 2pm several days a week in winter. During summer you can get information at the park services' Lily Lake Visitor Center (see "Visitor Centers & Information," in chapter 3). Information is also available online at **www.fs.fed.us/arnf**.

## SPORTS & OTHER OUTDOOR ACTIVITIES

**FISHING**    You'll catch rainbow, brown, brook, and cutthroat trout in the Cache la Poudre, the Big Thompson, and other area rivers. The national forest's mountain lakes, such as either of the two Lost Lakes, feature the same fish as the rivers, plus lake trout and kokanee salmon. Parts of the Cache la Poudre are designated Wild Trout waters; catch-and-release fishing and artificial lures and flies are required to protect the greenback cutthroat, the only local native trout. Also popular for fishing is Joe Wright Reservoir, located in the forest at 10,000 feet elevation, just off the northwest corner of the national park.

**HIKING**    There are hundreds of miles of trails leading to beautiful scenic areas, much like the terrain in the national park, but usually much less crowded. Here are two recommended trails, but there are plenty more. Check with forest service offices.

The 4-mile **St. Vrain Mountain Trail** is rated moderate to difficult. To get there, head south from Estes Park on Colo. 7 for about 18 miles to the community of Allenspark, and turn south on the dirt County Road 116. Follow it about 1.5 miles to a forest service sign to Meadow Mountain and St. Vrain Glacier. Turn right and go 0.5 miles to the trailhead parking area.

Climbing up into the alpine tundra, this trail takes you into Indian Peaks Wilderness Area and to the border of the national park. There are good views of Longs Peak, Mount Meeker, and the Wild Basin section of the park. From a forest of aspen and lodgepole pine, the trail climbs steeply up a glacial moraine, eventually reaching a saddle south of Meadow Mountain, with a 0.25-mile one-way side trip to the mountaintop. From this point it's about 0.75 miles to the western slope of St. Vrain Mountain. Once on top you get a 360° view of numerous peaks, and you should look for the St. Vrain Glaciers due west. The starting elevation is 8,800 feet, and the trail has an elevation gain of 3,362.

A shorter trail, the 1.5-mile **Lily Mountain Trail,** affords great views of several peaks inside the park, and this not-too-difficult hike is a terrific introduction to mountaineering for beginners. To get there, go south from Estes Park on Colo. 7 for 5.7 miles to the sign for Lily Mountain, and park on either side of the road.

The trail starts with a gentle climb to the north before switchbacking around to the south (at a junction—take the left fork) and follows several short switchbacks up a steeper incline amid boulders. As you climb, Twin Sisters Peaks become visible to the southeast. Look occasionally to the northeast also, where Estes Park and Lake Estes can be seen in the distance. The trail now becomes steeper and can be difficult to discern—watch for rock cairns marking the path. As it turns to the north for the final ascent, you'll be scrambling over boulders, still following the cairns.

On top, the views are magnificent in all directions. To the northwest is the Mummy Range, with Ypsilon Mountain, Mount Chiquita, and Mount Chapin on its left end, then Hallett Peak and Flattop Mountain to the west, and Longs Peak and Mount Meeker to the southwest. To the southeast are the Twin Sisters Peaks, and turning northeast you'll see Lake Estes and the results of man's intrusion into this magnificent land—the town of Estes Park. The initial elevation is 8,780 feet, and the elevation gain is 1,006 feet.

**HORSEBACK RIDING**   Many forest trails used by hikers are also suitable for horseback riding. Check with forest service offices for recommendations. To minimize the spread of non-native noxious plants, those taking hay into the forest for horse feed must be able to show that it is certified weed-free.

**MOUNTAIN BIKING**   Many, but not all, forest trails are open to mountain bikes; check with forest service offices. Bike rentals are available in Estes Park (see "Estes Park," above).

**RAFTING**   The ✪ **Cache la Poudre,** Colorado's only federally designated Wild and Scenic river, offers exciting whitewater rafting with serious rapids rated mostly Class III and IV. Fun for experienced boaters with good-quality equipment, this is not the place for on-the-job training, or for the use of those cheap little inflatable rafts from discount stores. First-timers will enjoy half-day trips with a licensed outfitter on

Class II and III sections, and there are half-day and full-day trips over Class III and IV sections that will bounce you around a bit more and are guaranteed to get you wet. Cost for half-day trips is $40 to $60 per person, full-day river trips are $80 to $90, and overnight trips cost $170 to $200. Among the area outfitters licensed to run the river are **Rocky Mountain Adventures** (☎ **800/858-6808** or 970/493-4005; www.shoprma.com) and **A-1 Wildwater** (☎ **800/369-4165** or 970/224-3379; www.a1wildwater.com).

## 4 Arapaho National Forest & National Recreation Area

Named for the Native American tribe that hunted in this area before the arrival of white settlers, this federal property includes the 36,000-acre Arapaho National Recreation Area, located in the vicinity of Lake Granby, just off the southwestern corner of Rocky Mountain National Park; and the much larger Arapaho National Forest, which spreads from the northwest to the southwest. There are also several designated wilderness areas within the forest boundaries.

As in Roosevelt National Forest, you'll find that regulations are generally less restrictive here than in national parks. Most trails (except those going into wilderness areas) are open to mountain bikes, and dogs are allowed on trails if leashed. In addition to hiking, mountain biking, horseback riding, fishing, and camping (see chapter 5), there are also abundant old mining and logging roads that offer opportunities for four-wheel-drive and motorbike excursions. Check with forest rangers for specifics.

### ESSENTIALS

**INFORMATION & VISITOR CENTER** For advance information, contact the **Forest Service Information Center,** 1311 S. College Ave., Fort Collins, CO 80524 (☎ **970/498-2770**). Information is also available from the forest service's **Sulphur Ranger District office,** 9 Ten Mile Rd. (P.O. Box 10), Granby, CO 80446 (☎ **970/887-4100**), off U.S. 40 about 0.5 miles south of the town. You can also get information online at **www.fs.fed.us/arnf**.

**FEES** Entrance into the national forest is free (except for camping), but the fee for entrance into the Arapaho National

Recreation Area is $5 per vehicle for 1 day, $10 for 3 days, and $15 for 7 days.

## SPORTS & OTHER OUTDOOR ACTIVITIES

**BOATING**   The biggest of the area's three major lakes, Lake Granby, located about 9 miles south of Rocky Mountain National Park's west entrance along U.S. 34, covers 7,256 acres when full, with about 40 miles of shoreline and a depth of over 220 feet. Several full-service marinas offer docking, mooring, fuel, boating and fishing equipment sales and rentals, and guided fishing trips. Power boats that can hold six people rent for about $200 per day; pontoon boats, which have capacities of 8 to 10 people, start at about $140 per day. Check with **Highland Marina,** 7878 U.S. 34 (☎ **970/ 887-3541;** fax 970/887-2261), on the west side of the lake. **Beacon Landing Marina,** on the north side of the lake, about 2 miles from U.S. 34 on County Road 64 (☎ **800/864-4372** or 970/627-3671), offers rentals and supplies, plus motel-type lodging units that start at $70 for two people.

**FISHING**   Although there are a number of rivers and streams in the forest, the best fishing is in the lakes. At Shadow Mountain Lake, just southwest of Grand Lake, you'll find several species of trout, including rainbows that are stocked from April through August. ◗ **Lake Granby,** especially when the water level is high, is a good choice for anglers seeking kokanee salmon and rainbow, brown, brook, and lake trout. The lake is stocked with rainbows and a small number of browns, and browns weighing up to 10 pounds are occasionally caught. Beacon Landing Marina (see "Boating," above) offers **guided fishing trips** that cost about $200 for one to three anglers for 4 hours; $300 for 8 hours.

**HIKING**   There are numerous hiking opportunities in the Arapaho National Recreation Area and Arapaho National Forest, including some that take you into the national park. The North Inlet Trail is an easy 2-hour walk to pretty Cascade Falls, and the East Inlet Trail is an easy half-hour walk to Adams Falls. (See trail descriptions in chapter 4.) There's an easy walk along the east shore of Shadow Mountain Lake (park near Greenridge USFS Campground and walk over the dam). Somewhat more challenging is the 3- to 4-hour hike to the top of Shadow Mountain, from which you have a spectacular view of the town, the valley, and all three lakes.

One popular trail is the easy mile-long ✪ **Bowen Gulch** self-guiding interpretive trail that winds through an old-growth forest. It was constructed in 1993 as a joint effort of the Forest Service, the Colorado Division of Wildlife, and the Colorado Mountain Club Foundation. It shows what old-growth spruce-fir forests look like, and illustrates the importance of this unique ecosystem for biological diversity. Among the wildlife that can be seen are voles, owls, goshawks, three-toed woodpeckers, and pine martens. The trail is closed to motorized vehicles, bikes, and horses, and it is located north of Lake Granby off a county and forest road. Get directions to the trail and pick up a brochure at the **Sulphur Ranger District office** in Granby, 9 Ten Mile Rd. (P.O. Box 10), Granby, CO 80446 (☎ **970/887-4100**), off U.S. 40 about 0.5 miles south of the town.

**HORSEBACK RIDING**    Many forest trails used by hikers are also suitable for horseback riding. Check with forest service offices for recommendations. To minimize the spread of non-native noxious plants, those taking hay into the forest must be able to show that it is certified weed-free.

**MOUNTAIN BIKING**    Many forest trails, except those in wilderness areas, are open to mountain bikes; check with forest service offices. Mountain-bike rentals are available in Grand Lake (see "Bicycling," under "Grand Lake," above).

**WINTER SPORTS**    Many of the trails in the Arapaho National Forest and Arapaho National Recreation Area are perfect for snowmobiling, cross-country skiing, and snowshoeing. However, some restrictions apply, especially to snowmobiles, which cannot be taken into wilderness areas, so check first with forest service offices.

# A Nature Guide to Rocky Mountain National Park

*P*icture-perfect scenery—rugged peaks capped with pure white snow, and a handsome bull elk standing proud against a deep blue sky—is usually the image that comes to mind when we think of Rocky Mountain National Park. However, beyond this pristine image lies a complex world, molded by extremes of temperature, moisture, wind, and especially elevation. In one section we find cactus, sagebrush, and similar plants of the desert, a wide range of wildflowers, and some of America's tallest trees. Beavers build dams, squirrels and chipmunks beg at roadside viewpoints, and jays noisily protest humanity's invasion of their home. But the park also houses an inhospitable realm of rocks and cold, where tiny plants survive by clinging to the ground for protection from bitter 100-mile-per-hour winds, and towering poles are erected to help road crews find the highway beneath the snow drifts when spring finally arrives. In short, the natural world of Rocky Mountain National Park offers much to those who would explore it on its own terms.

## 1 The Park's Life Zones

Elevation is the determining factor in locating and identifying the variety of plants and animals found in Rocky, and the park can easily be divided into three main zones: the montane ecosystem, at lower elevations; the subalpine, at the midlevels; and the alpine, at the park's highest elevations. The lines between the zones can be a bit fuzzy, and both plants and animals will cross boundaries at times. In addition, across these zones there are riparian areas, which are the wetlands adjacent to rivers, streams, and marshy areas. Within the 415 square miles (265,727 acres) protected by the national park are 17 mountains above 13,000 feet. Elevations in the park range from a low of 7,840 feet above sea level at the Beaver Meadows Visitor Center to 14,255 feet at the top of Longs Peak.

**Montane Zone**   In relatively low areas, usually below 9,000 feet, such as the areas near the Beaver Meadows Visitor Center, at Sprague Lake, and along the Gem Lake Trail, ponderosa pine and juniper cloak the sunny southern hillsides, and Douglas fir blankets the cooler northern slopes. The thirstier blue spruce and lodgepole pine cling to stream sides, where you will also find willow and cottonwood and the occasional grove of aspen. Wildflowers found here include larkspur, fairy slippers, western wallflowers, snowberries, and several types of daisies.

The warmest part of the park, because it is at the lowest elevation, the montane ecosystem has the greatest variety of wildlife. Elk and mule deer browse on sagebrush and bitterbrush, while Abert's squirrels dine on the ponderosa pine's seeds and twigs, and chickarees, also known as pine squirrels or red squirrels, harvest the seeds of the lodgepole pine. Coyotes and badgers frequent the open meadow areas, hunting squirrels and mice, and there are muskrats and beaver in the areas along streams and lakes. Watch for colorful mountain bluebirds, among the earliest of the park's seasonal residents to arrive, as well as the distinctive red-napped sapsucker, western tanagers, black-billed magpies, and warbling vireos, which can sometimes be heard singing from their nests in aspen trees.

**Subalpine Zone**   This sector lies between 9,000 and 11,500 feet elevation, such as the area around Bear Lake, at Glacier Gorge Junction, and near the Longs Peak Ranger Station. Forests of Engelmann spruce, subalpine fir, and limber pine dominate the landscape, interspersed with broad meadows that are vibrant with spring and summer wildflowers, including silvery lupine, shooting star, and Colorado columbine. In the lower sections of this zone, you'll also see aspen and lodgepole pine, especially where there has been a fire or some other disturbance to the forest.

Among the wildlife to watch for here are deer and elk, which graze on meadow grasses; beaver, which dine on aspen and other trees along the edges of lakes and ponds; chipmunks; and chickarees. Birds seen frequently in the subalpine zone include northern goshawks, Clark's nutcrackers, ruby-crowned kinglets, and both gray and Steller's jays. While most of these animals are found in other zones as well, the subalpine zone is the best spot to see the snowshoe hare and, perhaps, an elusive black bear.

The space between 11,000 and 12,000 feet, just below the tree line, is a transition area where trees called *krummholz,* a German word meaning "crooked wood," are found. Here the trees, predominantly spruces and firs, grow very slowly, and are stunted and deformed from the harsh, near-alpine conditions. Winds here are so ferocious that branches will often grow only on the trees' downwind side, giving them the appearance of banners or flags. The phenomenon is readily apparent as you enter this area on Trail Ridge Road.

**Alpine Zone**   Above 11,500 feet the trees become increasingly gnarled and stunted, until they disappear altogether. This is the alpine tundra. Tundra is Russian for "land of no trees," and fully one-third of the park is in this bleak, rocky world, where many plants are identical to those found in the Arctic.

Despite a short growing season of only 6 to 8 weeks, a variety of hardy plants survive here—some 200 varieties—most remaining small and clinging low to the ground for a bit of warmth, and to avoid being shredded by winds that routinely exceed 100 miles per hour. Many tundra plants contain the chemical *anthocyanin,* which converts sunlight to warmth, and some plants, such as the alpine sunflower, grow tiny hairs as protection from the elements.

Low grasses and sedges grow here, providing food for deer and other animals. You'll have to look carefully to see some of the alpine tundra wildflowers; their white flowers blend in with the patches of snow that remain in August. These hard-to-spot blooms include the Arctic gentian, Alpine lily, and alpine sandwort. Other species brighten the tundra during its short summers, including the purple fringe, deep-red king's crown (also called "roseroot"), purple sky pilot, blue alpine forget-me-nots, and golden draba, a member of the mustard family.

Animals that inhabit the alpine tundra include pikas, members of the rabbit family; yellow-bellied marmots; white-tailed jackrabbits; and northern pocket gophers, a favorite snack of coyotes and weasels. This area is also home to bighorn sheep, which have become a symbol of the park, and it is estimated

**Impressions**

*A world by itself in the sky.*
—Enos Mills, an early advocate for the establishment of Rocky
    Mountain National Park, describing the alpine tundra

that more than 200 elk—about one-third of the park's elk population—live in the alpine zone year-round. During the summer, birds to watch for include golden eagles, hawks, falcons, and white-tailed ptarmigans. Occasionally, a mountain bluebird also finds its way here.

## 2  The Landscape

Towering mountain peaks, snow-filled valleys, open meadows, and jagged rock sculptures fill the eye at Rocky Mountain National Park. Although the standard terrain-creating forces of uplift and water erosion that are responsible for the scenic beauty of much of the western national parks were key players here, another force that was not a factor at Zion, Bryce Canyon, and the Grand Canyon was also at work—glaciers.

Rock formations in the park are among the oldest in the United States, having been formed at least 1.7 billion years ago, when movements of the earth's crust created heat and pressure on deeply buried sediments that had been left from an earlier inland sea. This produced metamorphic rock, and then about 1.4 billion years ago volcanic activity deep underground created granite and other igneous rock. As the climate changed, shallow inland seas came and went, leaving deposits that over vast amounts of time became layers of sedimentary rock.

About 70 million years ago, a period of uplifting began in which big chunks of igneous rock, along with the younger sedimentary rock on top of it, fractured and were forced upward. Rivers carved away much of the sedimentary rock and began eroding the granite. Then, some 25 million years ago, volcanoes deposited more igneous rock on top of the older rock.

The earth's crust continued to shift and crack, lifting these layers of rock so that by about two million years ago, the peaks that form today's highest mountains were in place. Faulting and stream erosion continued, as earth movements fine-tuned the shape of the mountains, and streams dug V-shaped valleys.

Then Mother Nature got serious. The Pleistocene Ice Age arrived, temperatures dropped, and deep snow in the higher-elevation valleys was compacted into ice, creating glaciers that covered more than three-quarters of what is now the park. As the glaciers moved downhill under the force of gravity, they ripped into the sides of the V-shaped river valleys, transforming them into U-shaped valleys and carrying off rocks, dirt, and anything else that got in their way. Then, when the glaciers reached lower and warmer elevations, the ice began to melt, dropping the debris it had picked up on the way downhill. Geologists call deposits left along the sides of the valleys "lateral moraines," and deposits at the front of the glacier—its farthest point downhill—are called "terminal moraines."

At least four periods of glaciation occurred, interspersed with warmer, drier weather. The latest, a mere 28,000 years ago, is credited with creating the landscape in the Moraine Park section of the national park, where we can clearly see lateral moraines to the north and south, and a terminal moraine to the east. The remains of glacial deposits can also be seen in Glacier Basin, Horseshoe Park, and the Kawuneeche Valley; and Bear Lake was created when a terminal moraine plugged up a valley.

When exploring the park today, we see several billion years of geologic history. The oldest rocks—metamorphic and the earliest igneous rocks—form the higher elevations of Flattop Mountain and Trail Ridge. Younger igneous rock, some 25 million years old, can be seen at Lava Cliffs along Trail Ridge Road, on Specimen Mountain, and in the Never Summer Mountains. Both the Kawuneeche Valley and the valley where Estes Park is located were created by movements of the earth's crust some two million years ago.

Semicircular bowls, called "cirques," were formed at the tops of glacier-dug valleys. These are often filled with snow. There is a cirque on the side of Sundance Mountain, visible from Trail Ridge Road; and below the east face of Longs Peak, Chasm Lake is in a cirque. Grooves and scratches from glaciers, as well as glacial polishing, are apparent on rock surfaces along Old Fall River Road.

There are still a few small glaciers left in the park, although to most of us they're difficult to distinguish from patches of snow. You'll be able to see, at a distance, several glaciers from the Moraine Park Interpretative Trail, including Andrews, Taylor, Sprague and Tyndall Glaciers. Tyndall Glacier can also be seen from the Sprague Lake Nature Trail, and Andrews Glacier is visible from The Loch and Timberline Falls Trails. During wet years, Andrews Glacier shows evidence of movement down-valley, but it shrinks back in dry years.

A few areas of the park are the result of nonglacial erosion, and those can be seen along the Gem Lake Trail and in the Twin Owls area.

## 3  The Flora

The great variety of plants here—some 1,000 species—comes as a surprise. After all, a great amount of this park is in a land so bleak and so harsh that trees cannot grow at all. But even way up in the alpine tundra, close to 200 types of plants survive the long winters, bursting with color to make the most of whatever warmth the summer sun delivers. As you travel through the park, you will constantly be changing elevation, and as you do, the trees, flowers, and other plant life will change as well.

Of course, other factors also play a role in plant growth. The plants along the rivers and surrounding the park's 147 lakes differ from those on the rocky, high desert slopes. And because more rain and snow fall west of the Continental Divide than on the eastern side, there are different varieties of plants on each side of the park. Slope orientation is also important, with the southern-facing hillsides home to those plants requiring more warmth and sunlight than the colder north-facing slopes receive. One of the treats of visiting the park in midsummer is the abundance of wildflowers, and although the wildflower season usually peaks in late June or early July, you will find some species, such as orchids and columbine, that bloom practically all summer.

### TREES

**Colorado blue spruce**  These handsome trees are found at the lower elevations of the park, where they grow in small groves near water sources and sometimes in mixed forests.

Their sharp needles are silver-blue or deep green, and the trees can grow to over 100 feet in height with trunks up to 2½ feet in diameter. They have thin cones about 2½ inches long.

**Cottonwood**   A member of the willow family, cottonwoods like lots of water and are usually found along streams or other permanent water sources. The narrowleaf cottonwood, the species found in the park, grows at elevations up to 8,000 feet. It has skinny, pointed green willowlike leaves that turn dull yellow in the fall. Cottonwoods can grow up to 60 feet tall, with trunks about 1½ feet in diameter.

**Douglas fir**   This large evergreen—some can grow as tall as 200 feet, although most in the park are 100 feet or under—has medium-size blue-green needles and fairly large cones. It has a classic Christmas tree shape and grows primarily in the montane ecosystem. Birds and various mammals eat the seeds, while deer eat the foliage.

*Douglas Fir*

**Limber pine**   Found in the montane and subalpine zone, up to about 11,000 feet elevation, mature trees are fairly small, usually less than 30 feet, with a trunk diameter of 1½ feet. Also called the "Rocky Mountain white pine," these evergreens often have multiple trunks, and either light- or dark-green needles up to 2 inches long. In unprotected areas they often have a gnarled, twisted look. Look for them along Mills Lake Trail, growing seemingly straight up out of bedrock, and also on Emerald Lake Trail and along the shoreline at Gem Lake.

**Lodgepole pine**   This species—the most widely distributed pine in North America—typically grows tall and slender, losing its lower branches as they become shaded. Trees in the park, primarily in the subalpine zone, grow to be 90 feet tall, with trunks up to 1½ feet in diameter, and long yellow-green needles. This tree's name comes from the use of its straight, thin trunks as poles for tents and other shelters by Native Americans and white pioneers. It is also one of the first trees to appear after a forest fire because some of its seeds are not released until temperatures reach 110°. You'll see lodgepoles along East Inlet Trail, Cascade Falls Trail, and Twin Sisters Trail.

*Lodgepole pine*        *Ponderosa pine*

**Ponderosa pine**   This large, impressive evergreen, which is found in the montane zone, is easily recognized by its long needles—sometimes measuring more than 6 inches—that grow in bundles of two or three. Adult trees have orange-tinted bark that has a fragrance similar to vanilla, and large, reddish brown female cones that are round or egg-shaped.

**Quaking aspen**   This tree, which can be found growing from Alaska to southern Arizona, is found in the park at elevations up to about 10,000 feet. Its leaves, on long, twisted stems, shudder at the very idea of a breeze, hence the name "quaking" aspen. French trappers told a legend that Christ's cross on Mount Calvary was made of aspen, and that the quaking is the tree's trembling with shame. Its cool, downy-white bark feels great against your cheek on a hot day, and its almost-heart-shaped green leaves usually turn a striking yellow or gold in the fall. The trees can grow to 100 feet in height, with trunks up to 2 feet in diameter. Deer and elk browse the twigs, bark, and leaves, while rabbits and other small mammals eat the leaves, buds, and bark. Look for them along Trail Ridge Road, as well as along many park trails.

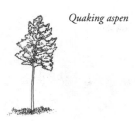

*Quaking aspen*

**Rocky Mountain juniper**   Growing in canyons and on rocky slopes up to 8,000 feet elevation, these junipers can sometimes reach 50 feet tall. They have slender branches and short gray-green needles, with berrylike cones that are a popular food for birds and other wildlife. The "berries" are bright blue with a white coating.

**Subalpine fir**   Also called "Rocky Mountain fir" and "alpine fir," this species grows up to 80 feet in height, with trunks over 2 feet in diameter; however, as they approach the tree line they are shorter and more shrublike. Growing in the park from 9,000 feet to 12,000 feet elevation, they have tightly packed dark-green needles, and their whitish bark is browsed by elk, deer, bighorn sheep, and moose.

*Subalpine fir*

## FLOWERING PLANTS

**Alpine sunflower**   The largest flower on the tundra, with blooms up to 4 inches across, this member of the sunflower family grows only in the Rocky Mountains. The plant's roots store solar energy for 10 summers or more before blooming once, and then it dies. For protection from the harsh climate, it grows tiny hairs, which have given it another common name, Old Man of the Mountain.

*Alpine
sunflower*

*Colorado
columbine*

**Colorado columbine**    Also called "blue columbine," this is
the Colorado state flower. A member of the buttercup family,
columbine come in a variety of intricate shapes and colors,
and nine species of columbine are found in Colorado. The
Colorado columbine is among the prettiest. Its flowers are
2 to 3 inches across, with five light-blue or white petals surrounded by five blue or purple petal-like sepals, or spurs. They
bloom from July through August, and are found in the montane and subalpine zones. Look for its rare relative, the dwarf
blue columbine, along the Twin Sisters Peak Trail.

**Elephant heads**    Found in wet areas at most elevations, elephant heads have stems up to 2 feet tall that sprout dozens of
what look like little pink elephant heads—complete with
floppy ears and a half-inch-long curling trunk. A good place
to see these flowers, also called "elephantella" and "little red
elephants," is on the Big Meadows Trail in the western section
of the park.

*Elephant
heads*

*Fairy
slipper*

**Fairy slipper**    Also known as the "calypso" or "calypso
orchid," it is found in the montane and subalpine zones and
is often seen among lodgepole pines in the Wild Basin section
of the park. It has delicate lavender-pink flowers and is one of

the earliest plants to bloom. The name calypso comes from the sea nymph in Homer's *Odyssey.*

**Fireweed**    Among the first flowering plants to appear after a fire, fireweed produces bright-pink flowers with four petals each. A member of the evening primrose family, it grows in the montane and subalpine zones, and it can be seen along the Grand Ditch and Ouzel Falls trails.

*Fireweed*

*Moss campion*

**Moss campion**    Also called "moss pink" for its delicate pink flowers, these plants hug the ground in moist areas in the park's alpine tundra, and they are sometimes found blooming in the protective environment of rock crevices.

**Mountain harebells**    Found in the montane and subalpine zones, mountain harebells are also known as "bluebells" and "bluebells of Scotland." They produce bell-shaped blue-violet flowers up to an inch long, and are usually seen in meadows or along rocky slopes. In Scotland, these plants are also called "witches' thimble," and it is believed the name harebell comes from the legend that witches could turn themselves into hares. A good spot to see them is on the hike along the shore of The Loch.

*Mountain harebells*

*Parry's primrose*

**Parry's primrose**    Attractive deep-pink flowers growing in clusters announce the presence of Parry's primrose in most areas of the subalpine and alpine zones. Watch for them along the East Inlet Trail to Lone Pine Lake and along Timber Lake Trail.

**Shooting star**    This member of the primrose family grows in the wetter sections of the montane and subalpine regions of the park. It has narrow purple flowers that grow up to an inch long, often with yellow at the base.

*Shooting star*

**Silvery lupine**    You'll see the purple flowers of the silvery lupine, a member of the pea family, in both the montane and the subalpine areas, often in forests of lodgepole pine.

**Sky pilot**    Named for where it grows—reaching toward the sky in the high mountains—the sky pilot's small five-petal purple or blue-violet flowers are found in the meadows of the alpine tundra and subalpine zones. A member of the phlox family, it has an unpleasant skunklike odor, and tiny hairs on its leaves and stem help reduce moisture loss and protect it from the harsh climate.

*Sky pilot*

**Snow buttercup**    A resident of the park's alpine tundra, these impatient plants are often seen pushing their small, bright-yellow blossoms up through the snow in spring.

*Yarrow*

**Yarrow**    Found at practically all elevations in the park, yarrow have clusters of small white flowers. A good place to see them is along the Coyote Valley Nature Trail in Kawuneeche Valley.

## SHRUBS AND SUCH

**Lichen**    These small, crusty plants—actually an algae and fungus growing together—are seen on rocks, where they produce a mild acid that helps disintegrate the rock's surface, turning it to soil where other plants can sometimes get a foothold. Lichens come in a variety of colors. Along the Bear Lake Nature Trail, watch for bright-orange lichen, created from nitrates either in the rock or deposited on the lichen by bird and mammal droppings.

*Big sagebrush*

**Sagebrush**    Covering much of the American West, sagebrush is found at the lower elevations at Rocky. A shrub that normally grows in alkaline soil in arid areas, it can reach several feet tall if it gets sufficient water. Browse for deer, elk, and other animals, sagebrush has a fresh, pungent scent—strongest when it's wet—that is similar to that of the spice sage. It has tiny gray-green leaves and sprouts small white flowers in the fall. The variety in the park is called "big sagebrush."

## 4   The Fauna

Many national parks have wildlife, and visitors to most parks will see a squirrel, a chipmunk, and maybe a deer or two. But the abundance of animals here, the larger mammals in particular, means that most park visitors will see dozens of elk and deer, bighorn sheep, and possibly a moose. Those interested in the smaller park inhabitants, such as rabbits and their cousins the pikas, squirrels and chipmunks, yellow-bellied marmots, coyotes, and a wide variety of colorful birds, will not go home disappointed. The extremes of elevation and temperature, Rocky's natural wildness, and the fact that the higher elevations are off-limits to most humans for more than half the year make this an ideal habitat for wildlife.

There are more than 60 species of mammals in the park, ranging from moose and elk that weigh well over 1,000 pounds to the tiny northern pocket gopher, which is seldom seen because it's busy digging tunnels and munching on roots underground. Bats also call Rocky home and feed over the park's lakes and ponds. There are more than 280 species of birds, 11 species of fish, and six amphibians, including the boreal toad, which is listed as an endangered species by the federal government. One snake—the harmless garter snake—and numerous insects, including a large number of butterflies, are also residents.

Although seeing wildlife is often the highlight of a trip to Rocky Mountain National Park, it is important to remember that these are wild animals, and not only can you harm them, but they can harm you as well. The park is not a petting zoo.

### Photo Tip

The key to getting good wildlife photos is to know the animals' habits, such as where they go and when. Get there first and quietly wait for your opportunity. Keep in mind that walking within photo or feeding distance of wildlife poses a threat to your well-being. It is not uncommon for elk in rut to attack unsuspecting shutterbugs. When the elk fills the viewfinder of your Telephoto lens, you're close enough.

## For Bighorns, Bigger Is Better

The symbol of Rocky Mountain National Park, bighorn sheep are named for the rams' large curving horns, which form an almost complete circle over 2½ feet long. Their most prominent feature, their horns play a major role in bighorns' lives. When settlers arrived in the area of the park in the 19th century, hunters quickly discovered that not only could they sell the bighorn's meat, but they also could get high prices for the male's horns. The bighorn population soon dropped from the thousands into the hundreds.

But it is not only humans that prize the ram's massive headdress. For the animals themselves it is a status symbol—the ram with the biggest horns gets all the females he wants. Unlike antlers, which are shed annually, horns are kept throughout the sheeps' lives. Females' horns grow only a small amount after the first 4 years, but males' horns continue to grow, usually reaching a magnificent curl by 7 or 8 years. After that the horns may exceed a full curl. When the large horns start to restrict the rams' peripheral vision, they sometimes deliberately chip off the tips.

Getting back to the important subject of these animals' sex lives, the rams are not especially particular, and will mate with any female in heat, often visiting other herds seeking additional ewes. During the mating season, which occurs in the fall, if more than one ram is following a particular ewe, the rams have butting contests, using their horns as battering rams and crashing into each other at speeds up to 40 miles per hour. These battles can continue for up to 20 hours, and the sound of horn hitting horn can often be heard over a mile away. However, these contests occur only between rams of equal horn size; those with smaller horns are out of luck.

There have been reports in recent years of visitors to the West's national parks being injured and killed by mountain lions and bears. Smaller mammals can carry and spread bubonic plague and other diseases. For instructions on how to conduct yourself in the park, see "Protecting Your Health & Safety," in chapter 2.

## MAMMALS

**Beaver**   These big rodents, up to 4 feet long and weighing up to 60 pounds, have fine, dark-brown fur, webbed feet, and a large black paddle-shaped tail. At Rocky Mountain National Park, they build dams, which turn streams to ponds and eventually to meadows. Fall is a good time to see beaver, usually in the evening in wetland areas throughout the park. Recommended viewing spots are near Glacier Creek Picnic Area, along Bear Lake Road, near the Endovalley Picnic Area, and along the road to the Cub Lake Parking Area.

*American beaver*

**Bighorn sheep**   The official symbol of Rocky Mountain National Park, bighorn sheep prefer rocky slopes away from humans but also frequent lakeshores, where they eat grasses and especially soil, which provides much-needed minerals. Ideally suited for life in harsh mountain climates, they have muscular bodies, excellent eyesight and hearing, a fine sense of smell, and hooves that are hard on the edges but flexible in the center, providing good traction on rock. They also swim well. The males (rams) can grow to over 300 pounds, while mature females (ewes) usually weigh no more than 200 pounds. Both sexes have horns. Female bighorn sheep are often mistaken for mountain goats, but goats are usually white, while bighorn sheep have tan or brown coats. There are no goats in the park. There were thousands of bighorns in the area in the mid-1800s, but the herds were decimated by hunters and ranchers who brought domestic sheep into the area, changing the bighorns' habitat and introducing scabies and pneumonia, which further reduced their numbers. By the 1950s there were only about 150 bighorns left in the area, but thanks to government protection and reintroduction efforts, herds are increasing; it is now estimated that from 650 to 800 live in and near the park. They are seen frequently at Sheep Lakes and Horseshoe Park from May to mid-August.

*Rocky Mountain
bighorn sheep*

**Black bear**   Rangers estimate that there are about 50 black bears living in the park's backcountry. Found throughout Rocky, they usually stay to themselves, avoiding humans, but during years when berry and nut crops and other food sources are low, bears will help themselves to whatever they find in backpackers' tents, packs, and even ice chests. Although often black in the eastern United States, black bears in the West are more frequently brown or tan. Males are big, measuring up to 6 feet tall and weighing over 500 pounds, but the females are much smaller. Bears' footprints look similar to those made by humans, with the addition of a small round mark above each toe, produced by the bears' claws.

*Black bear*

**Chipmunk**   A common sight in the park, often in open forests and meadows, chipmunks have brown and gray fur and black and white stripes on their backs, in addition to prominent black and white facial stripes. Of the 22 species of chipmunks in North America, 21 occur in the western United States. It is often difficult to tell one chipmunk species from another (at least for humans), but it's usually fairly easy to distinguish chipmunks from their cousins the squirrels, since chipmunks have facial stripes while squirrels do not.

*Least chipmunk*

**Coyote**   Seen throughout the park, but especially in open areas at lower elevations, coyotes hunt rabbits, rodents, and other small animals. Tan or yellow-gray, with bushy tails, coyotes look much like domestic dogs and usually weigh 30 to 40 pounds. They can run at over 25 miles per hour, reaching 40 miles per hour for short periods. One way to easily distinguish a dog from a coyote is to look at their tails—coyotes run with their tails down, while domestic dogs run with their tails up. Coyote choruses are often heard at night, consisting of a series of sharp yips, barks, and howls. Watch for coyotes along the Coyote Valley Nature Trail in Kawuneeche Valley.

*Coyote*

**Elk**   Also called "wapiti," the Shawnee word for a deer with white on its sides and flanks, Rocky Mountain elk are usually brown or tan, with hints of white or yellow on their rumps and tails. The males can weigh up to 1,100 pounds and stand 5 feet high at their shoulders, but they are best known for their antlers, which can reach 5 feet across and weigh 25 pounds. The antlers, which are shed each year between January and April, can grow half an inch per day. There are about 3,000 to 3,500 elk in the park during the summer, but that number drops to about 1,500 in winter, when the rest migrate outside the park. Elk are often seen in early evening shortly before sundown, and they are usually scattered about meadows along the roads.

There are more elk in Colorado than in any other state or Canadian province.

The best elk-viewing time is usually from mid-September to mid-October, during mating season, when amorous bulls compete for females, each bull gathering as many cows as possible. During this time, called "rutting," there is little actual fighting among bulls, but there is what is called "bugling," a call that warns other bulls to stay away. The sound starts low but soon becomes a shrill squeal or whine. Volunteers called the **Rocky Mountain National Park Elk Bugle Corps** are stationed at elk-viewing areas during rutting season to help visitors get the best views without disturbing the animals. Good spots to see the bulls gathering their harems each fall include Kawuneeche Valley, Upper Beaver Meadows, Moraine Park, and Horseshoe Park.

*Rocky Mountain elk*

**Moose** The largest relative of the deer, bull moose can weigh up to 1,600 pounds and stand 7½ feet tall at the shoulders. With long, dark chocolate-brown hair, they have poor eyesight, but good senses of hearing and smell. Usually seen alone or with one or two others, moose eat willow, aspen, and aquatic plants, and they can swim at up to 6 miles an hour. Known for an ornery disposition and unpredictable behavior, they are best observed from a distance and the relative safety of an automobile, although moose have been known to charge cars and even trains. The bulls are most aggressive during mating season, in the fall, and a cow becomes quite displeased if a person gets between her and her calf. Moose migrate in and out of the park's west side, and are sometimes seen among the willow along the Colorado River, the Big Meadows area, at the beaver ponds near Timber Creek Campground, and along the Onahu Creek Trail.

*Moose*

*Mountain lion*

**Mountain lion**  Also known as panthers, cougars, and pumas, these large cats are occasionally seen, usually on winter mornings, in the montane zone. Solid tan or beige, they prefer to eat deer, and a single mountain lion can kill and consume one mule deer a week if deer are plentiful. Weighing up to 200 pounds, they are exceedingly strong, and they also hunt elk, bighorn sheep, coyotes, beavers, small mammals, and birds. Mountain lions will usually stash the leftovers from their kills, covering them with brush, sticks, and leaves, for later consumption.

**Mule deer**  The park's mule deer are often observed in meadows along the edge of the forest. Considered medium-size as deer go, mule deer are usually reddish brown in summer and gray during the winter, with patches of white on their rumps and throats year-round. However, their most distinguishing characteristic—what has given them their name— are their huge mulelike ears. Bucks can weigh up to 450 pounds, while doe usually weigh only about one-third of that.

*Mule deer*

**Northern pocket gopher**   Named for their cheek pouches that serve as food storage containers, northern pocket gophers are usually grayish brown, with small dark eyes and tiny round ears. They grow to about 9 inches long. Rarely seen above ground, they are found throughout the park, including in the alpine tundra, and live in extensive underground tunnels, where they eat roots and tubers. Usually, the only visible evidence of their presence are long mounds of dirt signifying the location of their tunnel homes.

**Pika**   These small, cute, round-eared relatives of the rabbit—although they look more like guinea pigs than rabbits—like rocky slopes in the subalpine and alpine zones. They are often brown with some mottled gray coloring, and have no visible tail. Because they do not hibernate, pikas spend most of their time in summer gathering winter food. Much like a farmer, they cut grasses, lay them on rocks to dry in the sun, and then store their hoard in their lairs. Social creatures, pikas live in large colonies. They're quite vocal, communicating in a shrill sound that could be compared to that of a young goat. You can look for pikas along Old Ute Trail and the Grand Ditch Trail.

*Pika*

*Porcupine*

**Porcupine**   These slow-moving animals have large, chunky bodies, short legs, and sharp quills covering the back half of their bodies. The porcupine's 30,000 quills are modified hairs—hollow tubes with sharp, solid, barbed points—and they provide two functions: They discourage predators, and although the porcupine cannot shoot its quills, if attacked it will strike with its tail, driving the quills into the attacker's flesh, at which time the quills detach from the porcupine. The quills on the underside of the porcupine's tail also function as a brake to keep it from sliding down tree trunks. Porcupines can grow to 3 feet long and weigh up to 40 pounds. They like wetland areas and the subalpine forest. You might see porcupines, which are primarily nocturnal, along Coyote Valley Nature Trail.

**Snowshoe hare**   Found in the subalpine zone, snowshoe hares are known for their huge rear feet—their snowshoes—and the fact that the changing length of daylight as the seasons change triggers an altering of their hair color. In summer they are mostly a mottled brown, while in winter they become almost pure white. They eat grasses, berries, and the bark of aspen and willow. Seldom seen, these hares are especially shy, and when startled they will either try to hide in brush or run frantically, often in a wide circle, at speeds up to 30 miles per hour.

*Snowshoe hare*

*Albert's squirrel*

**Squirrel**   Practically every visitor to Rocky Mountain National Park sees squirrels. Species in the park include the golden-mantled ground squirrel, which digs complex tunnel systems under rocks. They have white stripes bordered by two black stripes along each side of their brownish gray bodies, and reddish brown or copper-colored heads and shoulders. These squirrels are often confused with chipmunks, which are generally the same size, shape, and coloring, but it's easy to tell them apart—chipmunks have stripes on the sides of their faces and golden-mantled ground squirrels do not.

Also in the park, often seen in the lower elevations of the Wild Basin area, are Abert's squirrels, easily identified by their long ears topped with tufts of hair. Also called "tassel-eared squirrels," they have white bellies and are dark gray above. Abert's squirrels usually live in the branches of ponderosa pines, where they eat seeds and twigs.

Chickarees, also known as red squirrels or pine squirrels, enjoy the seeds of lodgepole pines, and also eat a variety of other seeds and nuts, birds' eggs and young birds, and mushrooms, including species that are poisonous to man. Chickarees are usually rust red or grayish red on their upper bodies, and white or gray on the lower sections. They have rounded ears, bushy reddish brown tails with black tints, and measure up to 15 inches long. They're often seen, and their noisy chattering is often heard, along Coyote Valley Nature Trail.

*Yellow-bellied marmot*

**Yellow-bellied marmot**   A member of the squirrel family, yellow-bellied marmots are big—sometimes over 2 feet long and weighing up to 10 pounds—with golden brown fur on their sides and back, and a yellowish belly. They have bushy tails and live in rocky areas at higher elevations. Because they hibernate all winter, their main summer activity is fattening themselves up by gorging on whatever green vegetation is available. Sometimes they're called "whistling pigs" because of the high-pitched whistling or chirping sound they may make when startled. Look for yellow-bellied marmots along the Grand Ditch Trail and Old Ute Trail.

## BIRDS

**American dipper**   Also called "water ouzel," these year-round park residents are seen along streams, where they feed on insects and other aquatic life. In shallow water they appear to water-ski on the surface, but in deeper water they dive in and run along the bottom underwater. Mostly slate gray, with a stocky build and short tail and wings, the American dipper's loud call sounds like two stones being hit together. Watch for these birds along Ouzel Falls Trail and at the falls, where they dart in and out of the tumbling waterfall.

*American dipper*

*Broad-tailed hummingbird*

**Broad-tailed hummingbird**   These colorful little birds are delightful to watch as they hover at flowers to sip nectar, perform rambunctious aerial mating dances, or warn other hummingbirds away with tail-fanning and other displays. Hummingbirds are also the only birds known to fly backward. The most common of hummingbird species seen in the park, the broad-tailed hummingbird is a summer resident that will be found among aspen, Douglas fir, and pine trees, and near water courses.

**Clark's nutcracker**   Often seen along Trail Ridge Road and in the Bear Lake area, this year-round park resident is about a foot long, with a long light-gray hood, a white face, a pointed black bill, and black wings. Named for William Clark of the famed Lewis and Clark Expedition in the early 1800s, it eats the seeds of limber pines, which it pries from cones with its long beak, and is also not above begging or stealing food scraps from picnickers.

*Clark's nutcracker*

*Dark-eyed junco*

**Dark-eyed junco**   Frequently seen in many areas of the park, especially along the edges of forests, dark-eyed juncos are mostly gray, with black and white accents. Year-round residents of the park, they eat seeds and berries.

**Golden eagle**   These large birds, with wingspans usually over 6 feet long, are dark brown and black, with a light-gold color on the backs of their necks. Seen year-round in the higher elevations of the park, such as along Trail Ridge Road, they swoop down to grab rabbits and large rodents with their sharp talons. In flight, golden eagles are sometimes confused with turkey vultures, which are about the same size as eagles and are also seen occasionally in the park. The main visual difference is that the turkey vulture has a red head, and unlike the golden eagle, it can glide seemingly forever without flapping its wings, riding on columns of warm air known as thermals.

*Golden eagle*

*Steller's jay*

**Jays**   You are almost certain to hear a jay, because it is among the noisiest and most raucous-sounding of birds. Because of their size—sometimes a foot long—both Steller's and gray jays are easy to spot as well. Seen at numerous locations, including along Trail Ridge Road, Steller's jays are bright blue on their lower half and black on top, with a prominent crest on the tops of their heads. Gray jays, not surprisingly, are mostly gray, although their foreheads and parts of their lower body are white. They have earned the nickname "camp robber" because of their habit of carrying off whatever food they can find from camp and picnic sites. Gray jays like the subalpine zone and are often seen in the Bear Lake and Big Meadows areas. Both jays are year-round park residents.

**Mallard**   These large ducks, which can grow to over 2 feet long, like to paddle about on Sprague Lake and other water bodies in the park. Males have an almost iridescent green head, with a white neck ring, deep-brown chest, and light-gray body. Females, although attractive with mottled brown and black body feathers and white tail, are not as striking as the males.

*Mallard*

*Mountain bluebird*

**Mountain bluebird**   One of the most commonly seen birds at Rocky, and one of the most attractive, mountain bluebirds arrive early—usually in March. They like open meadows, aspen and pine forests, and even the alpine tundra. Males have bright-blue backs and tail feathers, and lighter blue chests; females are a duller gray-blue. They are often seen hovering low over the ground in search of insects.

**Mountain chickadee**   Year-round inhabitants, mountain chickadees are small—only about 5 inches long—and have pale-gray backs, jet-black caps and eye bands, and white cheeks, eyebrows, and chests. They're abundant in ponderosa pine and piñon-juniper forests.

*Mountain chickadee*

*Northern red-shafted flicker*

**Northern flicker**   Year-round residents of the park, although seen mostly in summer, northern flickers are large woodpeckers, up to a foot long, that are mostly brownish gray with a red band across the tips of their tail feathers. Males have a red strip on their lower face. They prefer woodlands of pine, Douglas fir, or aspen, and drill holes in these trees that provide homes for other species.

**Peregrine falcon**   With wingspans that often exceed 3 feet, peregrine falcons are one of the world's fastest birds, capable of diving at speeds over 125 miles per hour. Their backs and wings are usually slate gray or blue-gray, and this coloring projects vertically down their faces in bands over their eyes. The rest of their faces and necks are a light gray or white, and underneath, these falcons are usually a medium gray. Although they are not seen frequently in the park, they are occasionally spotted at higher elevations from spring through fall, and the park closes several rock-climbing areas to humans during the raptors' nesting periods.

Although pesticides drastically reduced the number of peregrine falcons in the United States in the 1950s and 1960s, they are on the increase again, thanks to the banning of those pesticides and successful efforts to raise the birds in captivity and release them into the wild. Peregrine falcons have also discovered cities, where they nest on tall buildings and bridges and dine on pigeons.

*Peregrine falcon*

**Red-tailed hawk**    Always on the lookout for small rodents, the main part of their diet, these year-round park residents are a common sight as they glide over open areas in search of prey, or perch in a pine tree at the edge of a meadow. Stocky, with wingspans of about 4 feet, red-tails are named for their rust-colored tails. Their chests and faces are usually white, and their upper parts vary in color, from light to dark brown.

*Red-tailed hawk*

*Violet-green swallow*

**Violet-green swallow**    Known for their long, pointed wings and superb grace while flying, violet-green swallows are pretty little birds, about 5 inches long, with striking metallic green backs, bright-violet tails, and white faces and lower extremities. You'll often see flocks of swallows soaring over the meadows and plateaus from spring through fall.

**Warbling vireo**    Often easier to hear than see, the warbling vireo is small—about 5 to 6 inches long—grayish green above and light gray or white below, with white eyebrows. Its slow song is rambling and easygoing, ending on a rising note. These birds are frequently seen during the summer in the park's aspen forests and in trees along streams.

*Warbling vireo*

*White-tailed ptarmigan*

**White-tailed ptarmigan**    Inhabiting the higher elevations of the park, about 11,000 feet and up, during the winter this year-round park resident roosts in small snow caves, which it digs with its chickenlike feet. At other times look for it near willow shrubs. During summer this bird, which measures about a foot long, is mostly mottled brown, with white wings, chest, and tail, but during winter it turns pure white.

## REPTILES & AMPHIBIANS

**Tiger salamander**    Looking much like a fish with feet, tiger salamanders can grow to be a foot long. They are found in the park's lower-elevation lakes, where they consume insects and aquatic creatures, but also will eat worms and small rodents.

*Tiger salamander*

**Wandering garter snake**    The only snake commonly seen in the park, this nonpoisonous species is found near streams at lower elevations. Usually brown and tan, with darker spots or stripes, these snakes can grow to be over 3 feet long.

## State Fish a Bit of a Wimp

Mistakenly believed to be extinct in 1937 and listed as an endangered species in the early 1970s, the greenback cutthroat trout has made a comeback, and in 1994 was named the official Colorado State Fish by the state legislature. It replaced the rainbow trout, a California transplant that had been listed on maps and other documents as the state fish, although state Division of Wildlife officials couldn't say why.

Known for its black spots and brilliant crimson color on its sides, the greenback cutthroat is one of four subspecies of cutthroat trout native to Colorado, one of the few species of fish that can truly be called the state's own. The greenback was abundant in Colorado waters during the early to mid-19th century, but pollution from silver and gold mining took its toll, and later the greenback was crowded out by the more aggressive rainbow, brown, and brook trout that had been imported to expand fishing opportunities.

Part of the greenback's problem is that it fails to live up to its cutthroat name, letting other trout invade its waters and practically jumping on any hook dropped into the water.

But rumors of its demise were premature, and two native populations were discovered just outside Rocky Mountain National Park in 1973. Efforts were begun to reintroduce the fish to its native waters, including park waters, as government agencies and Trout Unlimited provided it with places to live that are free from more aggressive newcomers. By 1978 its status had improved from "endangered" to "threatened." State wildlife officials hope that if the greenback continues to prosper it can be removed from the "threatened" list in the near future.

Today, the greenback cutthroat can be found in some four dozen bodies of water around the state, including Bear and Sprague lakes in Rocky Mountain National Park. Another good place in the park to see the greenback cutthroat close-up is from the boardwalks through the Beaver Ponds on Trail Ridge Road.

Although the greenback's designation as official state fish does not provide any additional protection, Division of Wildlife officials say it strengthens the public's willingness to protect the fish, and encourages anglers to throw it back if they catch it, as should be the rule with any threatened species.

## 5   The Ecosystem

To preserve and protect . . . and to provide for the enjoyment of park visitors.
—*National Park Service Organic Act, 1916*

As in most national parks, the primary threats to Rocky Mountain are being loved to death by increasing numbers of park visitors and air pollution from outside the park. A unique factor at Rocky that has both good and bad aspects is that large areas of the park are almost completely inaccessible for more than half the year. The challenge, of course, is for park officials to find ways to preserve the park's delicate ecosystems while still producing a rewarding experience for park visitors.

Practically all of America's national parks are suffering from overcrowding, although as Department of the Interior secretary Bruce Babbitt stated in late 1997, "The problem isn't too many people, it's too many cars." Park Service officials have taken the position that they do not want to limit the number of people who visit the parks, but rather they wish to manage park visitation to minimize the impact of tourism, not only on the park terrain and wildlife, but also on park visitors.

Mandatory shuttle-bus systems have been implemented during peak periods at especially crowded parks such as Grand Canyon and Zion, and although this is not yet planned for Rocky Mountain, officials say that they feel it is time to consider some type of alternative transportation system. The park service already operates a free, voluntary shuttle bus that runs up and down Bear Lake Road in summer, but no public transportation is yet available for busy Trail Ridge Road. Instead, park officials encourage people to avoid park roads at their most crowded times, driving them either early or late in the day, and to visit the park in late spring and early fall rather than at the park's peak season—the middle of summer.

The park's night sky—crystal clear with stars that appear so close you think you can touch them—has long been one of its attractions. But even though the park itself produces practically no air pollution, it cannot escape the pollution from vehicles driving into the park, development in its gateway towns—especially Estes Park—and the pollution from Denver, Boulder, Fort Collins, and other nearby cities. Air-quality monitoring, which began in the park in 1979, also indicates that the park's air is being affected by distant pollution sources, such as Los Angeles, Texas, and even Mexico. Park officials work with state and federal agencies to minimize pollution, but it is difficult to combat problems that sometimes originate thousands of miles away.

Although officials do what they can to spread out Rocky Mountain National Park's more than three million annual visitors, because Trail Ridge Road is fully open for only about 5 months each year, and sometimes less, the vast majority of park visitors show up then. It's hard to blame them—why go to a beautiful national park at a time you won't be able to see one of its most fascinating aspects, the alpine tundra? So no matter what park officials do to spread out visitation, and as much as visitors would like to go to the park when it isn't crowded, most tourists are going to be there at the same time. There is a plus side to this, though. The long, snowy winters protect the park's higher elevations, in essence giving at least the inaccessible alpine tundra back to its animals and plants.

Another issue facing park managers is ecological balance, and problems that at least in some cases have their roots in actions taken 100 years ago. This may sound like heresy, but Rocky Mountain National Park and the surrounding mountains may have too many elk. Stands of aspen trees that have existed since the last ice age are slowly disappearing, as browsing elk devour the young trees. This is an oversimplification, and a study is underway to determine all the causes. However, it appears that the area's elk are at least partly to blame. The elk population inside the park seems to have stabilized in recent years, but the number of elk outside the park has been increasing, in part because there are no wolves in the area to prey on the elk. Human hunters killed all the wolves in the area in the early 1900s.

Humans are also blamed for introducing the aggressive non-native plants that have made their way into the park and have choked out native species. Mostly from Europe and Asia, many of these blooms were brought to the United States and planted in the 1800s because people thought they were pretty. Plants such as leafy spurge can take over an entire meadow, not only by monopolizing water but by actually poisoning native plants. This plant is also toxic to wildlife. Park officials say that there are more than 100 non-native plant species growing in the park, and about a dozen of these are serious threats.

While efforts are being made to correct these mistakes from the past and to deal with outside problems such as pollution, one of the most effective ways to maintain ecological balance in the park, and to protect its wilderness, is by educating visitors.

Even at the height of the summer tourist season you can get away from humanity fairly easily by heading out onto park trails or into the backcountry, where you will find relatively unspoiled areas. To preserve these ecosystems, there is an increasing effort to make visitors understand the need for zero impact, or as close as people can get to that, short of staying home. In most cases, people are getting the message and are doing their best to stay on trails, to not pollute water or drop trash, and certainly to refrain from disturbing the park's plants and animals.

The issue of Rocky Mountain National Park's ability to handle an increasing number of visitors brings attention to the philosophy of the National Park Service, which essentially is to accomplish two goals simultaneously: preserving resources and promoting visitor enjoyment. Which is more important: protecting the plants, animals, and geologic formations that make America's national parks the special places they are, or helping people enjoy these very same plants, animals, and geologic formations? In an interview with the nonprofit National Parks and Conservation Association that was published in the November/December 1997 issue of the association's magazine, *National Parks,* park service director Robert Stanton said that resource protection should take precedence over the public's enjoyment. But he added, "It is a management decision to discern what level of visitor use can be accommodated without harming in an irreparable way the resources. . . . It's an easy thing to describe; it's a difficult thing to accomplish."